A YEAR OF
LIVING HAPPILY

A YEAR OF LIVING HAPPILY

WEEK-BY-WEEK ACTIVITIES TO UNLOCK
THE SECRETS OF A HAPPIER WAY OF BEING

LOIS BLYTH

CICO BOOKS
LONDON NEW YORK

Published in 2017 by CICO Books
An imprint of Ryland Peters & Small Ltd
20–21 Jockey's Fields, London WC1R 4BW
341 E 116th St, New York, NY 10029

www.rylandpeters.com

10 9 8 7 6 5 4 3 2 1

Text © Sarah Sutton 2013, 2015, 2017
Adapted from *The Secrets of Happiness* and *The Little Pocket
Book of Happiness*, both published by CICO Books.
Design and illustration © CICO Books 2017

A CIP catalog record for this book is available from the Library of Congress and
the British Library.

ISBN: 978-1-78249-477-5

Printed in China

Editor: Dawn Bates
Designer: Emily Breen
Illustrator: Amy Louise Evans

Commissioning editor: Kristine Pidkameny
Senior editor: Carmel Edmonds
Art director: Sally Powell
Head of production: Patricia Harrington
Publishing manager: Penny Craig
Publisher: Cindy Richards

CONTENTS

INTRODUCTION

Happiness is like a riddle. The more we want it and the more we seek it, the more elusive it becomes. And yet, when we are least conscious of looking for it, it can envelop us in a warm sense of contentment and belonging, making a single moment precious and valuable beyond measure.

A feeling of happiness has the power to light up our whole being. It is elemental. It can be triggered by the smallest event. Scientists will tell us that it has the power to heal and to extend life. It is the ingredient we all seek to make our lives complete. Like the air we breathe, we are not conscious that we need it, until it disappears. Happiness makes us feel glad to be alive.

CHOOSING HAPPINESS

Why are some people happy and others not? People may be healthy and wealthy beyond measure but still feel discontented or unhappy. Are we born happy? Can we learn to be happy? Where does it come from and how can we live happier and more contented lives? There is no single path to happiness, because everyone views the world slightly differently, and each person's road to contentment is unique.

The happiness habit is an easy one to acquire. The difficult bit for some is choosing to step away from *un*-happiness and deciding, wholeheartedly, and with total commitment, that happiness is something that they really do want—and that they deserve. The challenge for others is choosing to step out of the place of comfort and familiarity and to start experiencing new challenges that inspire them to live their life in a different and vibrant way.

Much has been written about the power of positive thinking and the way it can help areas of the brain literally to rewire over a period of time; but for positive thinking to become a new habit you first need to let go of the negative thoughts that may have become a mainstay of getting by, up until now.

Our moans, groans, and grumbles may seem very innocent individually. If they have become an ingrained habit, you may not even realize that they are there, but their impact over a long period can be devastating. Negative thoughts train your brain to think negatively. These thoughts will affect your choices and your actions, and their outcomes, because they have an impact on the way you see the world. Over time, they have the power to steal our capacity for joy in life. The yearbook that follows has been created to help you or someone you care about, to take stock of the good things in life—and take positive steps to reclaim a happy future.

"VERY LITTLE IS NEEDED TO MAKE
A HAPPY LIFE; IT IS ALL
WITHIN YOURSELF IN YOUR WAY
OF THINKING."

MARCUS AURELIUS (121–180 CE)

Happiness requires you to adopt a new way of seeing the events in your life, involving a willingness to let go of the past and to recognize that things don't happen *to you*—they just happen. And they happen either because you helped to make them happen, or because you just happened to be there at the time. Personal disappointments and tragedies can have such a profoundly numbing effect that it is possible to put your life on hold—for years. But even in our darkest hours we can choose to see the glimmer of light that tells us there is joy to be had, in every situation, and there is the promise of a happier outcome, if we choose to look for it.

This book has a simple mission:

- To offer hope to those who feel that happiness is eluding them.
- To offer ways of thinking about the state of happiness that can create a sense of joy and contentment.
- To encourage those who are happy to value, share, and discover more ways to live a truly fulfilled and enjoyable life.

HOW TO USE THIS BOOK

The introductory pages that follow explore some of the science behind happiness and why happiness is within everyone's grasp— you just have to choose it! Then there is an activity for you to do each week of the year, including background information on how it can help to bring more happiness into your life. If you miss a week, don't worry—this is meant to be fun, not a chore! Whatever works for you will be the right way to continue. There is no need to do the exercises sequentially. This is not a program—it is a creative place to explore your ideas and feelings. There are notes pages at the end of each week where you can record your thoughts and feelings about that particular activity and a checklist at the end of the book to help you to keep track. Maybe you can share some of the ideas with loved ones too and spread a little happiness throughout the year!

"IF YOU WANT HAPPINESS FOR AN HOUR; TAKE A NAP.
IF YOU WANT HAPPINESS FOR A DAY; GO FISHING.
IF YOU WANT HAPPINESS FOR A MONTH; GET MARRIED.
IF YOU WANT HAPPINESS FOR A YEAR;
INHERIT A FORTUNE.
IF YOU WANT HAPPINESS FOR A LIFETIME;
HELP SOMEONE ELSE."

CHINESE SAYING

THE SCIENCE OF HAPPINESS

Scientists have finally proved it—happiness is good for you. Those who are happy or have an optimistic and positive outlook are far less likely to suffer from clinical depression. Happiness appears to lead to a longer life, greater health, and increased levels of resilience.

Scientific research into the effects of happiness has an impressive pedigree. Aristotle pondered the causes and impact of happiness as long ago as 322 BCE. He suggested that the pursuit of happiness was an essential part of being human, and a goal in itself.

More recently, scientists have discovered something that they call the "Happiness Paradox"—the more intent you are on pursuing solely your own path to happiness, the less likely you are to feel happy; whereas the more willing you are to focus on and help other people with no thought of your own gain, the happier and more content you will be.

There is another paradox: even though the standard of living has increased in most Western countries over the past 30 years, national levels of happiness have not increased at all.

THE FORMULA FOR HAPPINESS

The pursuit of happiness is part of our identity as human beings. For Americans, it is part of national identity too, embedded in the heart of the United States' Declaration of Independence. The Declaration, signed after a long period of war and disagreement, confirmed the desire of the 13 States to become independent of the British Empire. Part of the US government's responsibility to the people remains, "to effect their Safety and Happiness." At government level, the concept of happiness is synonymous with a desire for freedom.

In the early 1970s, 34 percent of people in the UK described themselves as "very happy." By the late 1990s, at a time when the country's economy was buoyant, the figure had dropped 4 percent. The improved standard of living across the country appears to have had a slightly negative effect on the nation's happiness.

Nor are people in the UK quite as neighborly as they used to be, with 43 percent saying that neighbors are now less friendly than they were ten years ago, and only 22 percent saying their neighbors are friendlier now. But overall, they are a pretty contented bunch. A UK Happiness Formula poll found, in 2005, that 92 percent of people described themselves as either fairly happy or very happy. Only 8 percent said they were fairly or very unhappy; and over 60 percent spoke to up to five friends each week. It seems that the happiest country in the world is Switzerland, followed by Denmark, Sweden, Ireland, and the USA. Britain comes eighth.

On the one hand, the statistics are interesting and provide food for thought; they are the stuff of future government policies and social science surveys. On the other hand it feels slightly absurd to think that happiness can be measured and verified. Surely there can be no completely reliable way to measure people's feelings?

It is encouraging to know that governments around the world are now setting policies that factor in the importance of happiness, but at the end of the day, no matter what the statistics say, each individual in every house, street, college, and office has the power to determine the collective optimism of a nation as a whole.

"HAPPINESS IS LIKE A BUTTERFLY; THE MORE YOU CHASE IT, THE MORE IT WILL ELUDE YOU, BUT IF YOU TURN YOUR ATTENTION TO OTHER THINGS, IT WILL COME AND SIT SOFTLY ON YOUR SHOULDER."

BUDDHIST PROVERB

GROSS NATIONAL HAPPINESS (GNH)

High in the Himalayan mountains, nestled between the borders of India and China, lies the Buddhist kingdom of Bhutan. It is not a wealthy country, and it has a range of social and economic problems, but the people have been described as the happiest in the world. This is partially due to the influence of the fourth king of Bhutan, Jigme Singye Wangchuck, who came to believe that a country should be measured not only by economic success, but also by the level of contentment of its people. He traveled widely and was attending a conference in Havana when a journalist from India asked him about Bhutan's Gross National Product (GNP). The monarch is reported to have replied, "In Bhutan, we don't care about Gross National Product, we care about Gross National Happiness."

He went on to establish GNH as official government policy. It aims to balance spiritual and material care in the areas of social development, cultural preservation, conservation, and good governance. The Bhutanese people now have free health care and free education. Since the scheme was launched in 1978, life expectancy has increased by 20 years and household income per capita by 450 percent. Happiness really is something to smile about in Bhutan.

DEVELOPING A HAPPY BRAIN

We know very little about the human brain—or more accurately, an extremely small percentage of people in the world, who have trained as neuroscientists, know a great deal about the brain in comparison with the rest of us. In fact, their understanding has doubled in the last 20 years, but by their own admission, the brain remains the last frontier of the human body.

Interestingly, every new discovery seems to find more evidence of the brain's plasticity; its ability to adapt and reinvent itself over time. Playing an important role in this is the front area of the brain, known as the prefrontal cortex. This is a uniquely human feature. It allows us to develop free choice, helps us to develop a sense of right or wrong, helps us to regulate our emotions, and it is a large part of who we are.

What has all this got to do with happiness? The brain is changing all the time and as we change our mind, so we strengthen or weaken the connections between the cells in the brain known as neurons. The neurons send messages along pathways. The more we repeat a thought, whether positive or negative, happy or sad, the stronger the pathway becomes. Our thoughts, like most people, prefer to take shortcuts. It is rather like cutting a corner across a grass verge. The first time someone does it, barely a footprint is left on the grass, but if everyone else takes the shortcut too, it won't be long before a new pathway has been forged.

A greater level of brain activity in the left side of the prefrontal cortex is associated with positive emotion and well-being. This side of the brain puts the brakes on negative

"FOR EVERY MINUTE YOU ARE ANGRY YOU LOSE SIXTY
SECONDS OF HAPPINESS."

RALPH WALDO EMERSON (1803–1882)

thinking. So if you practice positive thinking on a regular basis, the neural pathways in the brain that are associated with positivity will strengthen.

The flow of various neurochemicals in the brain varies from time to time. Interestingly, when people practice gratitude in a conscious way, the levels of reward-based "happy" hormones, such as dopamine, are increased.

Love, too, stimulates the brain in a positive way. Someone in love only needs to look at a picture of their loved one for the parts of the brain associated with positivity and rewards to become more active.

There is now evidence to show that where we focus our attention can consciously change the way we think. If we draw our attention to all the things that make us mad and angry and unhappy, and hang on to those thoughts, we will strengthen their power. If, on the other hand, we choose to reframe the negative into something positive, or focus consciously on positive and happy memories, then those are the neurons that are going to be strengthened.

Those in the field of alternative health have known about this for years, but now a body of evidence is developing, drawn from the results of clinical trials.

"HAPPINESS IS NOT A GOAL ...
IT'S A BY-PRODUCT OF A LIFE WELL LIVED."

ELEANOR ROOSEVELT (1884–1962)

HOW TO HAVE A HAPPY PLANET

The New Economics Foundation recommends five happy things to do each day to keep your happiness quotient healthy. It is the happy equivalent of eating your greens:

- Connect with those around you, and recognize the people in your life who are the cornerstones of your well-being.
- Be active. Find a form of movement and exercise that you enjoy and do it regularly—go for a walk, spend time outside.
- Pay attention to the world around you and the beauty that surrounds you.
- Keep learning. Take up a new subject; rediscover an old passion; repair your bike; sign up for a course; learn a musical instrument.
- Give your time, money, warmth, a smile, a gift, friendship—anything that will add to other people's lives and help to motivate them to do the same.

The Foundation has also devised an innovative method of measurement that assesses the connection between ecological efficiency and well-being around the world, and assesses results, country by country. Known as the Happy Planet Index, it uses data based upon life expectancy, experiences of well-being, and the ecological footprint of each country.

The results show that consuming high levels of natural resources does not result in high levels of well-being. In 2017, a new edition of the *World Happiness Report* showed Scandinavian countries (topped by Norway) to be the happiest in the world, based on subjective perceptions of levels of freedom, generosity, social support, healthy life expectancy, and trustworthy governance. The UK and USA fall below The Netherlands, Canada, New Zealand, and Australia.

KNOW THE SYMPTOMS

The symptoms of happiness are easy to spot, especially in children. Cries of laughter, big smiles, the desire to run, jump, shout, and try new things are all symptomatic of the joyous impact of being happy. Whether experienced as a short burst of laughter, or a life full of joy, happiness is powerful and its impact is contagious.

The symptoms of being less than happy are also contagious. They take hold more slowly, but may last for longer and show up in many ways. Have you smiled at yourself in the mirror lately? Did the smile come easily, or did it feel as if the muscles in your face need a little exercise? You don't need to reach a full-blown state of unhappiness to be aware that you would prefer your life to be more joyful, more relaxed, or more fulfilling. The signals show up in body language and the things we do and say. How often have you heard a less-than-happy person say, "I wish …," "I should have …," "If only …," "I can't because …," "You're lucky …," "I'm so tired …" followed by a frown and a deep sigh? It is wise to try to immunize yourself against the power of negative thoughts before you are exposed to them; or to boost your levels of positive thinking if you know you have come into contact with them.

The danger is that discontent can become a familiar reflex. It is all too easy to drift along in a state of grumbling dissatisfaction, sometimes for years, blaming circumstances, waiting for something to happen, and finding every excuse not to make the changes that could transform life and make you happier.

The common signs of chronic negativity are:

- Reproachfulness. You may blame yourself, your family, your job, your circumstances, for the way you are feeling about yourself and about your life.
- Regret. You may have a general sense of sadness; suffer feelings of worry and loneliness; feel unlovable, let down, or generally disappointed with life, your friends, or your achievements.

- Anxiety. You may feel overstretched, worried, or worn down by responsibilities and the demands of others.
- Self-defeating behavior. You may be snappy and bad-tempered, feel a lack of personal motivation, and have a history of overeating, smoking, or drinking too much, or taking too little exercise; then feel sorry for yourself because of health problems or financial worries.
- Becoming isolated. Everyone has personal demons and self-destructive habits that jeopardize happiness from time to time; people tend to tuck themselves away when they are unhappy. Those negative feelings and behaviors can also be flags of distress, signaling "help me" while simultaneously pushing away the very people who care about you.
- Premature aging. Discontent and unhappiness show up on the body. Unhappy people slump more; they seem to have more wrinkle lines, from frowning so much; they may neglect their appearance, so hair, teeth, nails, and clothes look tired.

BLUFF YOURSELF HAPPY!

The good news is that you don't have to start happy to become happy. The moment you begin to smile, laugh, relax your shoulders, and wipe away the furrowed brow, two interesting things happen:

- The brain responds by releasing endorphins, which are the attraction hormones, and oxytocin—the "cuddle" hormone—making you feel instantly more positive, relaxed, and attractive.
- Those around you will behave more positively.

The result is that the brain learns to become happy, even if you didn't feel that way to begin with. The other secrets of happiness can be easily learned, too. Practicing them over time will see you through tougher times and carry others with you.

CHOOSE HAPPINESS

Happiness is as invisible as electricity, and just as powerful. We can feel its effects and see its impact, but everyone's description of what it does will be different. When happy people smile or speak, their radiance can light up a room. Their warmth makes everyone more tolerant of others' views and foibles. When we are happy, we glow and we are beautiful, and more things feel possible.

But happiness can be turned off very suddenly, as surely as blowing out a candle. The moment we choose to invest importance in things that are outside our control, we put our happiness at risk. We begin to focus on what we want, and when we do not get it, we feel disappointment, or a sense of loss and failure. If the goal or desire is important to us and is closely aligned to our sense of who we are as individuals, it can be hard not to feel diminished when things don't quite turn out as planned. In low moments it can feel as if happiness will never return.

What can we do to turn things around? How is it that some people are able to live their lives with contentment, no matter what life throws at them, while others are left buffeted and devastated by disappointments and feel constantly let down by life. Every life includes periods of sadness and disappointment. Darkness and grief have a way of throwing shadows when we shine light upon their surface, which conjure up self-doubt and imaginings. Unhappiness can send ripples across the years and trigger other memories; the current loss may remind us of all losses; the current "failure" may turn the whole of life into a failure. Each disappointment may have a physical and personal impact long after the cause of the original sadness has been consigned to history.

The danger when we are in the grip of grief or sadness or despair is that in our determination to be independent we build walls around ourselves that are so high others cannot reach us. Not only are we without happiness, we are alone. For a minority, the pain that this causes can be catastrophic. They will turn to ways to numb that pain rather than sit with it a moment longer.

DEVELOPING RESILIENCE

Developing the habit of conscious optimism can shore us up for more challenging times. As we grow in resilience, so we grow in understanding. As Eleanor Roosevelt once said, "A woman is like a tea-bag. She won't know how strong she is until you put her in hot water." And the same is true of men.

When a life is rocked by a series of misfortunes or tragedies, it is inevitable that the person who is suffering will cry out to themselves, "Why me?" It is only human, and necessary, to come to terms with what's happening. But beware of becoming trapped by a sense of personal injustice that will prevent you from moving on.

If you choose to believe that your life is unfair, you will find it hard to be happy, because, in effect, you are telling yourself that you are powerless and that life has made you a victim of circumstance. In giving away your power in such a way, the danger is that you are also giving away your sense of self. As Viktor Frankl observes in his remarkable book, *Man's Search for Meaning*, even in the most dire of circumstances it is still possible to choose our attitude and retain our sense of identity.

> "EVERYTHING CAN BE TAKEN FROM A MAN BUT ONE THING: THE LAST OF THE HUMAN FREEDOMS—TO CHOOSE ONE'S ATTITUDE IN ANY GIVEN SET OF CIRCUMSTANCES, TO CHOOSE ONE'S OWN WAY."

VIKTOR FRANKL

CHOOSING THE BRIGHT SIDE

For many people the most powerful way to transform a sense of helplessness is to make a plan and take control; or to gain insight by focusing on other people's needs instead. Offering kindness to others can be a powerful way to redress the balance and change perspective. Conversely, there are other times when we need to "surrender" and let go of control, instead seeking acceptance and trusting that "this too will pass."

Choosing to look on the bright side may sound like a platitude—and may seem difficult to achieve—but the new and brighter moments are usually there, and always worth the hunt. The path to happiness lies in our capacity to see the bigger picture, through positivity, hope, and compassion for others.

EVERYONE DESERVES HAPPINESS

In our darkest hour lies a deep-rooted fear that somehow happiness will remain elusive forever. But that need not be so. Everyone deserves happiness—it is within everyone's grasp.

THE SPIRIT OF HAPPINESS

Happiness is essential to our spiritual well-being, and a relationship exists between levels of happiness and involvement in spiritual practice. The path to spiritual happiness has nothing to do with material gains, and everything to do with seeking inner peace and understanding. In prayer, or contemplation, or meditation, a primary goal is to let go of negativity and attachment to emotions that prevent us from feeling compassionate toward one another—and ourselves.

All forms of spiritual practice and religion emphasize a connection between spiritual fulfillment and happiness. The ability to live life with conscious self-reflection is a key part of the process of learning on the path to fulfillment. There is another common theme, too—the quest for the happiness and well-being of all our fellow humans.

Just as the repetition of positive thoughts will reprogram the neural pathways of the mind to think more positively, so, too, the spiritual rituals of happiness have been used over centuries to fine-tune the mind—and the heart. The process of prayer in all its forms opens us up to the possibility of Universal love and awakens us to our greater purpose.

Spiritual teachings include the concept of forgiveness, because only by finding a way to forgive ourselves and others can we learn from our mistakes and develop and grow as human beings. Since earthly happiness is less than perfect; all spiritual traditions share the belief that the ultimate state of bliss will be attained in the next life rather than this one.

"MY MAIN COMMITMENT IS... TO ACHIEVE A HAPPY, SUCCESSFUL LIFE... FOR A HAPPY, SUCCESSFUL LIFE, MUCH DEPENDS ON OUR MENTAL ATTITUDE, OUR MENTAL OUTLOOK."

THE DALAI LAMA

WEEKLY ACTIVITIES

Discover happiness week by week with a range of simple activities that you can easily incorporate into your everyday life. The note pages throughout can be used to record your thoughts and feelings at the end of each section, developing over time into your personal happiness journal.

LOOK FOR HAPPINESS

When we look back over the course of our lives, it will not be the detail of the profit and loss sheet, the pressure of deadlines, or the escalating cost of groceries that you will remember—it will be the great times with friends, the joy of watching your children in the school play, a special day in a beautiful location, the joy of walking your dog, the first time you heard your favorite piece of music, shared moments with loved ones. Even in times of crisis, it is possible to find something to laugh at, or something to appreciate—when we pay attention.

Writers and artists will often keep notebooks or draw sketches of things that have caught their attention. My wonderful mother kept a "thinks book" well into her eighties to capture her memories of the past and record each day's events that give her pause for thought. The inner journey that we travel in life has the potential to be endlessly rich and varied; it provides opportunities to explore and develop our true selves in a way that can open up our minds to new opportunities, who we are, and what we might be.

OUR TRUE SELVES

Blogging, tweeting, and other social media have their role to play but sometimes, when we share our thoughts with the world, we offer the edited version. We present ourselves as we would like to be seen, rather than revealing what we really feel.

Keeping a happiness journal can be a wonderful way of tuning in to the here and now and reminding yourself to pay attention to the present. You can, of course, use this book itself: there are note pages throughout and at the end of the book. Getting into the habit of writing down, photographing, painting, or capturing in some way those moments when you have felt alive, content, or joyful has several benefits:

- You will immediately feel the experience more intensely, as you seek to capture it.
- Your happiness radar will increase its powers of detection. The more you look, the more you will see reasons to be happy.
- It will serve as a record of happy moments and as a pick-me-up for those times when you feel blue.
- It will encourage you to think beyond the experience of the moment, to make connections between different experiences, and to learn more about yourself.

Of course, over time, some of the things that have brought you joy may also turn out to be a source of sadness as you recall times gone by, but the value of capturing the moment when it's fresh is that you can remind yourself of how you felt on that day—and treasure the memory.

THIS WEEK... Start a happiness journal

Each day of this week note down three things that have brought you joy and pleasure. Some examples might be:

- A beautiful aspect of nature
- Something that made you smile or laugh
- An act of kindness you experienced or heard about
- Delicious food
- An activity you enjoyed

Try to express how you felt at that moment and include photos in your journal whenever you can.

REFLECT... ON LOOKING FOR HAPPINESS

_____

_____

_____

_____

_____

_____

_____

_____

_____

_____

_____

_____

_____

_____

_____

_____

_____

_____

_____

_____

_____

_____

_____

LIVE SIMPLY

Happiness expert Srikumar Rao believes that we spend most of our lives learning to be unhappy instead of enjoying the pleasure of feeling vibrantly alive. This is because we spend so much time thinking about what we have to get before we can be happy; and because we tell ourselves we have failed if the outcome is not exactly as we expect it to be. We tell ourselves IF we have a better job, more money, a nicer house, a more attractive partner, a better car, THEN we will be happy.

The flaw in this argument, as he points out, is that anything you get, you can also lose—at which point not only are you are left without it, you also become unhappy, and you probably blame yourself for the loss.

As long as we are attaching importance to things external to ourselves—and as long as we are intent on criticizing the present and contrasting it with an idealized future—we will always be discontented. The closer we get to our destination, the more we will want to upgrade to something else, so will never reach the place where happiness is. We will never truly see and appreciate what we already have.

Contrast this with the way we feel when we see a beautiful rainbow, or a sunset, or something of beauty in the natural world. The effect on most people will be to "stop and stare" and to experience a moment of stillness and wonder. In Rao's words, in that moment of appreciation you are truly happy because, "You accepted the Universe exactly as it was," with no hint of criticism or wishing it was somewhere else or somehow different.

WHAT'S REALLY IMPORTANT TO YOU?

If you had only 24 hours left on this earth, would you go shopping or would you want to spend time with those you care about?

Money can't buy happiness, although it can, of course, buy fun, thrills, and enjoyment in the short-term. The culture of acquiring possessions, home-making, and dressing well is rooted deep within our psyche and very few people would be willing to give it all up and to choose a non-material way of life in order to achieve happiness. However, material possessions are passive. They cannot love us, or talk to us, or make us laugh— but they do have the potential to leave us comparing what we have with others, and so may feed dissatisfaction, encouraging us to feel that nothing will ever be enough.

The natural pleasures that we enjoy for free make us happy without dissatisfaction or judgment. It is enough that they are there. These are the riches that make us truly happy; and this is the kind of happiness that makes us truly rich.

THIS WEEK... Appreciate your life

Take time, right now, to consider all the non-material things that you have to be grateful for. During the course of your life, what or who has made you smile, laugh, feel loved, feel alive, feel curious, feel happy?

- Are you thinking about your love of music, running, climbing, singing, reading, dancing?
- Are you appreciating your friends, your family, your lover, your children?
- Are you remembering places you have visited, the beauty you have seen, the air you have breathed?
- Are you imagining the joy of a kiss, a scent, a taste, or a feeling?
- Are you treasuring a memory of someone no longer here?

REFLECT... ON LIVING SIMPLY

_____
_____
_____
_____
_____
_____
_____
_____
_____
_____
_____
_____
_____
_____
_____
_____
_____
_____
_____
_____

FIND HAPPINESS AT WORK

How happy are you in your work? Do you love what you do or is it simply a means to an end? Is there a boundary in your life between your time working and your time of leisure, or is there a seamless continuation, where work and play are one and the same. Does your work fire you up with enthusiasm, or drain your energy?

There is great joy to be had in working hard to achieve something, or putting in effort to earn a reward. Few people would look around at the home they have created, or consider the task they have completed, or the exams they have passed, and think to themselves, "I really wish I hadn't had such success!" Most people are justifiably proud of their achievements and the effort that went into reaching the outcome. Achievement is inspiring. Moments of celebration lift everyone's spirits. Good news helps others to think about what is possible, too.

Nowhere is this more obvious than in sport or adventure. When the first man on the moon, astronaut Neil Armstrong, died, thousands of adults recollected the impact the moon landings had had on their own lives. When millions of people around the world watch the Olympic Games, they are united in their desire for their favored competitor to win. Success, like so many of life's experiences, is enriched when it is shared. Why, then, are so many successful people unhappy and dissatisfied with their lives? Why, when we strive so hard to be successful, does it not always bring us joy? Why do so many successful people consider themselves to be failures?

Darwin told us that the future of all species depends on the survival of the fittest; from birth we are rewarded for things we do well and are encouraged to be the best we can be. In the work place, results are rewarded with a promotion or a pay rise. Human beings are naturally competitive, and striving to become "the best we can be" can bring great prizes. We become extremely attached to our achievements. They define us.

A SLIPPERY SLOPE ...

Here are some of the reasons why many of us become dissatisfied in our work:

- Fear of failure may lead us to play safe, leading to boredom and a lack of personal growth.
- Over time, our work goals and our life goals may start to conflict rather than support one another.
- We may become detached from the task, or may dislike or resent it.
- We may continue in a profession because we are good at what we do, and it is comfortable, rather than because we feel joy in our work.
- If we lose status or are made redundant, we lose our sense of self, because so much has been invested in the role. It can take years to build up confidence and self-esteem once again.
- Many people under pressure at work feel that they need to carry the weight upon their shoulders and do everything themselves. They feel they can't ask for help. They overlook the fact that asking for help is a strength, and that the greatest successes are achieved as a team.

Rather than investing in an outcome over which you cannot possibly have full control, the secret of happiness is to focus instead on the process of achievement, recognizing that each step is an achievement in its own right, and each marks progress on the way to reaching your ultimate goal. The key to getting a better job is first to focus on the one you have and to do it to the best of your ability.

THIS WEEK... Change your mindset

The pathway to finding happiness at work begins in the mind. Try this exercise both to change your mindset and discover what kind of work would make you happier.

- Before you go to sleep each night, find something positive to say or think about going to work in the morning and write it down. It doesn't matter how large or small that thing is. It need have nothing to do with the work itself; you might enjoy the journey to work, bantering with colleagues or being paid at the end of the month. Whatever it is, write it down.

- When you wake up the following day, pay attention to how you feel about going to work. Is your first thought positive or negative? If it is positive, write it down. If it is negative, read the positive thought you had last night and think again. Can you swap your positive for a negative? Write that down. Even extreme negatives can be reframed into positives. Instead of "I hate my job," try thinking, "Knowing how unhappy I am in my work shows me that I would be better suited to work that is ..." (Only you can fill in the gap.)

- Think about each task that you have to complete during each day and focus on how good it feels to complete each one. Acknowledge to yourself how well you have done and consider how you could do it even better next time.

- If you keep this up over the period of a month, three things will happen. First, you will have a list of things that make you feel happy and positive about your job that you will have repeated every day; second, you will notice more things about your work that you enjoy, which will make you feel happier at work, and will make others react more positively toward you. Thirdly, if you are still unhappy, you will know much more about what kind of work would suit you better.

REFLECT... ON FINDING HAPPINESS AT WORK

_____

_____

_____

_____

_____

_____

_____

_____

_____

_____

_____

_____

_____

_____

_____

_____

_____

_____

_____

_____

CHANGE YOUR LENSES

Shawn Achor is author of *The Happiness Advantage* and CEO of Good Think Inc. His work turns the conventional success formula on its head. Rather than hard work delivering happiness and satisfaction, he believes that happiness increases our capacity for hard work.

His study of the connection between our levels of happiness and its direct effect on our productivity has had an impact not only on individuals but also on companies and on the world of finance. He has spoken to business leaders in over 45 countries, offering them evidence for how happiness benefits productivity and the state of the economy.

During the course of his work, Achor has discovered that the majority of people spend a great deal of time focusing on competition, hassles, disadvantages, and problems rather than paying attention to the positive advantages and opportunities that they might have. We need to change the lenses through which we view the world in order to reframe our impressions with a more positive perspective.

In a simple experiment, he has observed that if people develop the habit of writing down three new things that they are grateful for every single day, that simple act will have a positive influence on the way their brains work in just three months. Thinking positively sends out ripples of influence that offer the world the opportunity to be happier—exponentially.

When we are happy, we are more productive; when we are positive in the present moment, our brains are able to work more effectively. When we are happy, our levels of dopamine increase naturally, which infuses the brain with a more positive way of viewing the world.

VALUE WHO YOU ARE

We live in a world where office workers choose to undergo minor cosmetic enhancements during their lunch hour; where celebrities of every age pay extraordinary amounts to get their breasts, buttocks, noses, and other body parts restructured, when no one else had noticed their presumed flaws. Thousands of people around the world who are blessed with beauty are unhappy with the way they look and think that losing weight, gaining weight, buying a designer sweater, or changing their hair color will somehow make them feel better about themselves.

Children as young as ten are suffering from eating disorders. What on earth is going on? Have we reached a point where we value looks over substance? Youth over aging? At what point did beauty start to mean everyone has to try to look the same?

On one level, this complex subject is quite simple—we cannot physically see ourselves as others see us. We see ourselves only when we look in a mirror or look at a photograph. How can we notice the light in our eyes when we are looking out of them, not into them? How can we see the energy in our step when we are inside our body?

HOW WE ARE REMEMBERED

Each of us is a unique human being, and we are changing both physically and emotionally all the time. The chances are that no one will remember in five years' time what color dress you wore to a particular event; or whether your hair was too long or too short. They may not even remember what you said. What they will remember is whether they enjoyed your company and whether your company made them feel good about themselves, too.

The person who lights up a room is not the one who is the most physically beautiful, but the one whose inner light brightens the lives of those around them. The truth in the myth is not that "If I were more attractive, I would be happier," but "If I were happier, I would be more attractive." That starts with valuing yourself for who you are.

THIS WEEK... Look back

I challenge you to:

- Delve into an old photo album that you haven't looked at in years and take a fresh look at the photos of yourself when you were 10 years younger. How attractive did you feel then? The chances are you felt the same way as you do now, but in looking back you will see how lovely you were. Were you any happier with your appearance? Probably not.

- Now imagine how you will react in 10 years' time when you look back at photos of yourself today, and do the same exercise again. Really feel it.

- Next, look in the mirror at your present-day self and smile as if you are looking at someone you care about. Look at the lines around your eyes that tell the world how you smile; look at the lines that tell the story of your life; and look at the way your face lights up when you smile. Your older self can look back in appreciation at how beautiful you are right now.

REFLECT... ON VALUING WHO YOU ARE

_____

_____

_____

_____

_____

_____

_____

_____

_____

_____

_____

_____

_____

_____

_____

_____

_____

_____

_____

LET GO OF FEAR

There are times in life when we need to risk all to gain happiness, while also letting go of some aspect that feels familiar. Strange as it may seem, sometimes the hardest thing to let go of is the safety blanket called fear. Fear encourages us to stay put, to remain risk-averse. It is the voice in your ear that tells you, "It's not worth the risk," and, "It's better not to try than to fail." By so not doing, you are in danger of forfeiting the opportunity and living a life filled with regrets.

The pathways to happiness appear in many guises, and not all of them are immediately recognizable as ways you would want to venture down. They may look strange, too unfamiliar, too full of obstacles, too far away from home, too frightening. But happiness is closely related to feelings of positive self-worth and achievement. We need to take calculated risks in order to grow and develop self-respect.

Life's milestones are turning points that encourage us to take stock because there is a choice to be made, or something is about to change that means nothing will ever be the same again. It may be a milestone of achievement; a birthday that marks a new decade; a moment of loss and grief; or a new chapter that is simultaneously exciting and terrifying.

In these moments, we measure where we are against where we expected to be, and compare what we have achieved with what we originally dreamed of for ourselves. They are brave moments that challenge contentment and shake up the future.

MAKE SPACE FOR HAPPINESS

Happiness is a large emotion, full of life. It doesn't thrive in situations where over-thinking stifles action, or where resentment and disappointment close the heart to the possibility of feeling joy. Somewhere between lost dreams and reality are thoughts you can dwell upon, steps you can take, and choices you can make that will dispel unwanted fears and turn potential regrets into opportunities for growth and change.

Much has been written about the "comfort" zone—that familiar space we operate within from day to day; and the "stretch" zone—where we learn new skills and develop new competencies. With competence comes confidence, which boosts self-worth and self-esteem. Inspirational business coach and trainer Bev James often reminds her clients that unless we find the courage to step into the stretch zone, we will be forever wondering what life might have held, if only we had been a little braver.

The roots of fear lie in the mind and in our memory. Fear is the body's way of protecting us from real or perceived threat. Anxiety triggers the adrenaline response and increases blood flow to the heart, in preparation for "fight" or "flight." Developing the happiness habit helps you to identify your thought triggers, so you can get to the source of the fear—and understand what makes you truly happy.

THIS WEEK... Challenge your fear

The following activity is a modified version of Bev James' approach. (See her book *Do It! or Ditch It* for more detail.) Ask yourself:

- What am I frightened of? Is it a fear of something real, or something imaginary. (The mind cannot differentiate between the two.)
- What is motivating me to act and what might be holding me back?
- What do I have control over so I can change it?
- What do I have no control over so I will have to accept it?
- On a scale of 0 to 10, how happy will my decision make me?
- Will my decision lead me to step toward or away from further happiness?

REFLECT... ON LETTING GO OF FEAR

_____
_____
_____
_____
_____
_____
_____
_____
_____
_____
_____
_____
_____
_____
_____
_____
_____
_____
_____
_____
_____

GOING WITH FLOW

Mihály Csíkszentmihályi (pronounced Me-Hi CheekSENTme-Hi-e) has had a huge influence on our understanding of what it means to be happy through his work on a concept he calls "Flow." He is one of the world's leading experts in the field of positive psychology.

When we are in flow, we stop feeling conscious of time because we are so absorbed in the task. The results of our work seem to come through us rather than from us.

Csíkszentmihályi has identified the conditions that are needed for flow, which include:

- A sense of being involved in the task.
- A feeling of being outside the bounds of everyday reality.
- A sense of clarity and focus—we know what we are doing and where we are going.
- Taking on tasks that we have the skill level to complete.
- Having the discipline to concentrate on what we are doing.
- A sense of timelessness—of being so involved in the task that we are not aware of time passing.

His work has clarified that for a task to be satisfying, it needs to be challenging, but within the scope of our abilities. If there is too much stress involved, productivity diminishes; if it is too easy, the motivation to do the task drops. Flow is the opposite of apathy—it drives us to act with purpose. When we are in flow, our sense of self is suspended, although completion of the task reaffirms self-value and provides a sense of satisfaction for work well done.

HUG MORE!

Scientists tell us that the roots of self-esteem stem from the earliest stages of our life. According to Sue Gerhardt, author of *Why Love Matters*, the unconditional love that we receive as babies appears to influence brain development. Babies who are comforted when they cry learn to soothe themselves as they grow; whereas babies who are left to cry develop a highly sensitized response to stress, which means that they find it harder to manage stress when they are adults.

But why is this? When we are stressed or feel in danger, the body produces a hormone called cortisol. We need a certain amount of cortisol, but in high stress situations, we produce too much, too often, which can have a tiring effect on the body and leave people less able to manage their emotions. Those who are highly sensitive to stress will try to self-soothe—for example, by eating high carbohydrate foods.

The good news is that getting physical with someone else will reduce your stress levels, reduce your cortisol levels, and increase the production of oxytocin, a "happy" hormone, in the body. All of this will make you feel happier, and will also boost your immune system.

THIS WEEK... Get physical!

Make a special effort to try some or all of these:

- Hug a friend
- Get a massage
- Comfort a baby (but ask the parents first!)
- Hold hands with your loved one
- Stroke the dog
- Cuddle the cat
- Make love
- Go dancing

REFLECT... ON HUGGING MORE

_____
_____
_____
_____
_____
_____
_____
_____
_____
_____
_____
_____
_____
_____
_____
_____
_____
_____

COMMUNICATE CONSCIOUSLY

The barriers to personal happiness are often the same barriers that block effective communication. So often we think we are paying attention, or making ourselves understood, when the opposite is true.

Making someone feel acknowledged, heard, and respected is the greatest gift of happiness that can ever be bestowed. As the good saying goes: you have one mouth and two ears—make sure you listen twice as much as you speak!

When we tune in to what people are really saying, we feel more strongly connected and more compassionate. When we feel heard and understood we feel more loved, better supported, more contented, and we are more likely to listen to and help others.

Smiling draws people toward you. It is a gift of positive intention. When you smile at someone, you make them feel welcome and good about themselves. One person's happiness can lighten the mood of a whole roomful of people. As the saying goes, "A smile is contagious—pass it on!"

THIS WEEK... Take the 10 ways test!

Below are ten ways to communicate with very few words, but genuine engagement. By trying to incorporate as many of these into your week as you can, you'll notice a difference in your relationships with friends and loved ones.

- Smile
- Communicate with your eyes
- Show your enthusiasm
- Engage with interest
- Put your cell phone on mute
- Pay full attention
- Be sincere
- Respect differences
- Simply LISTEN
- Show gratitude

REFLECT... ON CONSCIOUS COMMUNICATION

SHAPE UP FOR HAPPINESS

What if, instead of going to the gym to exercise, we were going to the gym to become happier? What if, instead of running on the treadmill to lose weight, we were told that running on the treadmill would improve our friendships? Would this help increase membership numbers? It would be good to think so!

Exercise is good for you in more ways than one. It tones your body, keeps you healthy, and it boosts your mood, which in turn helps self-esteem and self-confidence. And let's face it, when we feel good about ourselves, we feel happier too, which leads to a positive frame of mind.

As little as 30 minutes of exercise has been shown to lift a depressed state or enhance happiness and self-confidence. Exercise is a great way to lift your mood and balance your emotions. Exercise is often team-based and competitive, which appeals to those whose achievements affect their happiness levels. It also triggers physiological changes within the body and the release of "happy hormones."

CHANGING YOUR ATTITUDE

"But I hate exercise," I hear you say! Hating exercise is like saying you hate being able to move your arms and legs. Exercise is easy. It is what we were designed to do. You

just need to keep increasing the amount and speed you move your body, each day. You can also quite simply think about your posture. Having the right posture and tuning into your body can make a big difference to how you feel. The body holds tension. When we feel anxious, our breathing becomes shallow and our shoulders rise. By taking deep breaths and shaking out the shoulders, you will release tension, improve your posture, and immediately feel lighter and happier.

Taking up exercise doesn't mean you have to sign up to a gym or run a 5-kilometer race. Even walking the dog or a brisk stroll around the block a few times a day is a good start. The heart is a pump, which needs to be exercised to work at its best. When the blood is circulating properly around the body, it supports all the essential organs of the body, and clears out the waste and toxins. It increases the level of oxygen to the body and brain.

EXERCISE FOR HEALTH AND HAPPINESS

The Cochrane Review is the most influential review of its kind in the world. It has produced an analysis of 23 studies on exercise and depression. Their results showed unequivocally the impact that exercise has on lowering the incidence of depression. Exercise was shown to be as effective as antidepressant medication in helping to reduce mental symptoms.

Controversy remains about whether exercise leads to improved mental well-being, or whether those with positive mental well-being are more likely to exercise—but for anyone non-medical, the message is the same: Exercise makes you happier.

Science tells us that those people who exercise at least two or three times per week experience significantly less depression, anger, and stress than those who exercise less frequently or not at all.

- If you are feeling a bit low, a quick 20-minute burst of exercise can change your mood and raise your happiness levels.
- Those who do battle with depression are encouraged to exercise for 30 minutes per day for a minimum of 3–5 days each week.
- I once worked with a highly successful entrepreneur who said she was caught doing star jumps in an office corridor while waiting for an interview. It was her favorite way to overcome anxiety.

Exercise can help you achieve many different goals:

- "I want to feel calmer and happier." If you are feeling uptight or angry, exercise will help to release tension.
- "I feel overwhelmed by my problems." Many people, including business leaders and politicians, go walking or running when they have to think through a problem.
- "I want to lose weight and look great." Many people lose weight through exercise rather than going on a diet.
- "I want to look younger." Exercise keeps the blood healthy and helps the skin to renew and replenish old cells. It will help you sleep better too, all of which adds up to a more youthful and energetic you.

SET REALISTIC GOALS

The world tends to be divided between those who love to exercise—and those who prefer to talk about why they should exercise. When you are wearing your exercise "Learner" plates, short-term goals that include the "happy factor" are more motivating than long-term goals. For example, telling yourself, "It's a beautiful day for a walk and the fresh air will clear my head"; is more motivating than "I must go for a run around the block, it will lower my cholesterol."

THIS WEEK... Choose to begin

Don't worry about how much exercise you take—just make a start. Once you're out there doing it, you might just be surprised at how enjoyable it is!

- Get on your bike!
- Dance yourself happy.
- Go for a short jog—combine walking and running at first.
- Take the stairs, not the lift.
- Offer to walk a friend's dog.
- Park your car further away and walk part of the journey.

REFLECT... ON SHAPING UP

_____
_____
_____
_____
_____
_____
_____
_____
_____
_____
_____
_____
_____
_____
_____
_____
_____
_____
_____
_____

SLEEP WELL

Various research studies have found a direct correlation between getting enough sleep and being happy, yet many people let a busy life get in the way of going to bed at a reasonable hour. Unlike animals, humans will actually deprive themselves of sleep!

A US 2015 survey of more than 7,000 adults found that those who had slept for the recommended 8 hours per night reported greater well-being than those who had less sleep than this. The average well-being score for those who had eight hours sleep was 65.7 out of 100, compared to 59.4 for those who had six hours.

THE NEGATIVE EFFECTS OF SLEEP DEPRIVATION

Lack of sleep can affect your life adversely by:

- Making you irrational, clumsy, and more likely to make mistakes. You literally can't think straight if you haven't had enough sleep.
- Affecting your relationships: you're more likely to be irritable and unreasonable.
- Making you more likely to think negatively.
- Slowing your responses, making you less alert, and affecting your memory.
- Increasing your chances of becoming physically ill.
- Adversely affecting your physical appearance.

THIS WEEK... Make sleep a priority

Plan sleep into your weekly routine to boost your health and sense of well-bring.

- Set yourself a bedtime that will give you preferably eight hours sleep a night.
- Turn off your tech—including the TV—an hour before bedtime.

- Plan your food and drink around your bedtime, making sure you don't eat too late into the evening or consume caffeine after 3pm.
- Get up at the same time each morning, including at the weekend.

REFLECT... ON SLEEPING WELL

AVOID THE MOAN ZONE!

It usually takes no more effort to think a cheery thought than it does a gloomy one, and yet many people spend less time being consciously happy and more time focused on grumbling—about the weather, the traffic, the lack of parking, their boss, their partner, their lack of finances, their children.

When someone says, "Hi. How are you?" what do you reply? It probably depends on your age, your nationality, how well you know the person, and your frame of mind. Often the question is more an extension of "Hello" rather than a genuine enquiry into the state of someone's health. Occasionally, people will take the enquiry literally (usually when you are in a tearing hurry) and spend the next half-hour offering a blow-by-blow account of their latest medical history. (Well, you did ask …) But commonly there will be a long-suffering sigh followed by, "I'm fine," "Mustn't grumble," 'Bearing up," "Surviving," or some such phrase. What does that really mean? Would people say that if they were truly happy? Probably not. Would people feel happier if they said instead, "I'm great thank you; never better!" The chances are, they might.

IT'S CONTAGIOUS!

The grumbling habit is normal for many people, and it can be insidious. The more you complain, the more you notice to complain about, and then others around you start to grouse, too. Conversations become a grumblefest of grumble one-upmanship. "You think you had a terrible time on your vacation, just let me tell you about what happened to us …" "I know just what you mean, I had the same problem the other day …" "The government is terrible," "The town has changed," "Things used to be so much better." And so it goes on …

Happy people are less likely to grumble. They tend to notice the good in things first, and welcome the opportunity rather than notice its failings. They "choose to do" things rather than "decide not to do" things. Grumblers tend to look for faults, whereas happy people accept, or adapt. Happiness embraces opportunity and praises achievement. It creates an environment where better things become possible and joy is appreciated.

THIS WEEK... Tune in to yourself

If when you speak you tend to put a dampener on things, you may find that people tune out from what you say and may even avoid your company. Listen to yourself and try to change the way you think about and respond to things. You will start to see things differently and immediately feel happier.

- Listen to yourself talking in the same way you would listen to a GPS system. Imagine what it would be like to have a grumbling GPS while on the vacation of a lifetime. The sun is out, you are feeling relaxed, the car is packed, and you are ready to explore new territory. But every time you reach a road junction or turn a corner there is a complaint, a sigh, or an expression of regret from your Grumble Positioning System. "What a shame you didn't go left there," "This junction is always a pain," "I get so tired of being stuck in traffic," "The café we passed an hour ago was so much nicer than the one you are stopping at." Your mood would sink; your enjoyment would plummet. You would probably turn it off and go back to map reading.

- Try instead to say something positive first, before the negativity kicks in. Laugh at the things that annoy you and try to see the possibility instead of the problem. The chances are that those you are talking to will follow your lead and echo your mood with a positive reply.

REFLECT... ON AVOIDING THE MOAN ZONE

_____

_____

_____

_____

_____

_____

_____

_____

_____

_____

_____

_____

_____

_____

_____

_____

_____

_____

_____

_____

_____

_____

BECOME LESS COMPLACENT

Many of us don't realize how happy we are because we take our current life so much for granted. We are always looking for faults and wishing for something else. Familiarity and routine threaten the specialness of what we have right now.

Most children and teenagers are blissfully complacent, especially those who have grown up with the material comforts of the western world. They take their education for granted; they expect to be fed; most will know that they are loved; and many will have clothes, gadgets, or vacations paid for by those who care for them. Children deserve to feel secure and safe until they are ready to make their own way in the world. It is part of the deal. Very often it is not until children have left home for the first time, or started families themselves, that their sense of appreciation really begins.

But if the pattern continues through life—getting without giving, receiving without reciprocation—both the giver and the receiver are left in a place of disadvantage. Complacency shows in a lack of awareness of others and an absence of gratitude. It is perfectly possible to have fun and be complacent at the same time in the short-term, but in the long-term, those who are complacent about their friendships, relationships, or material comforts without safeguarding them may lose them altogether.

Even those who have had a difficult life need to be alert to complacency. Being aware of what it feels like to be neglected or overlooked can help us to appreciate the value of care and kindness, and encourage us not to be complacent in learning how to treat others better than we are treated ourselves.

DO SOMETHING DIFFERENTLY

Memory expert Tony Buzan says that the mind tends to remember things that are different, not things that are the same. So if your routine is unchanged day to day, you will begin to become complacent, because you will no longer notice what you are doing. Making the effort to do things differently occasionally, or swapping responsibilities, or saying thank you with a surprise gesture, will stay in the mind for longer and have a greater impact.

THIS WEEK... Give thanks

Look for ways to be grateful and show appreciation for what you've had and have in life.

- Remember who has helped you. Is there anyone who has shown you support and care who you have forgotten to thank or acknowledge? Are there people in your life who are always there for you, to the point where you take them for granted? When you consider the path that your education and your career have taken, who has helped you along the way?

- Say thank you for the small things. Saying thank you, especially for the things we receive as a matter of routine, each and every day, is the easiest and kindest way of making someone feel loved and appreciated. A spontaneous thank you, a big smile, plenty of eye contact, and perhaps a hug can make the dullest chore the happiest task in the world.

- Give before you get. We don't need a reason to show someone we care about that we appreciate them. Be spontaneous and show someone how much you care before they have done anything for you.

- Walk a mile in another man's shoes. Experiencing the world from another person's perspective is guaranteed to help us to understand them better and appreciate what we ourselves have.

REFLECT... ON BECOMING LESS COMPLACENT

_____
_____
_____
_____
_____
_____
_____
_____
_____
_____
_____
_____
_____
_____
_____
_____
_____
_____

STOP PROCRASTINATING

Procrastination is the thief of time—and it will steal your life, too, given half a chance. Procrastination is a major enemy of happiness because it will never allow you to plan ahead with confidence, relax without guilt, or produce your best work. Procrastinators miss out on parties, vacations, tax breaks, and even having children, because their dread of deadlines means they haven't been paying enough attention to how they prioritize their time.

The art of chronic delay is worry dressed up as fear and accessorized with avoidance, pain, and guilt. Any pleasures in the life of a procrastinator feel stolen surreptitiously, because wherever you are and whatever you are doing, you know you should really be somewhere different, doing something else instead.

Chronic procrastinators feel full of self-loathing because they know they disrupt other people's lives with their delays. In letting others down, they let themselves down too. Whatever the original cause (and there are many different reasons), the underlying problem is the strong belief that they can never be anywhere or get anything done on time. Of course, that is far from the truth.

Many procrastinators seek their pleasures in gratuitous diversions. Drawers will be tidied efficiently at the moment they should be getting dressed for work; crossword puzzles are completed at the moment a letter should be written; someone else's problem is solved at the very moment they should be prioritizing their own. A common problem for a procrastinator is the inability to say no. Another is having an unrealistic idea of how much they can achieve in a day.

But the greatest one of all is a misplaced belief that they are hopeless, and the consequent tendency to focus more on their fear of the finish date while paying no proper attention to when or how to start.

SCHEDULING

"To do" lists are torture for a procrastinator, because they seem to get longer and longer every day, but a well-planned schedule can become a thing of joy and a route to happiness. Draw it, create it in Excel, but map it out in such a way that you can pin the printed-out version on your wall and see it all the time. Set up reminders in your online diary if it helps—but the trick is to have something in front of you as a visual reminder of what actions to take at every moment of every day.

Two important points are worth bearing in mind:

- Don't use the actual deadline as your scheduled deadline. Make sure the deadline that you list on your schedule is a good two weeks (or more) ahead of the formal cut-off. This is the golden rule. If necessary, leave the real date off your schedule altogether, so your brain is not distracted by it.

- Highlight your START dates in a brighter color than your finish date, and tick them off as you go. Most schedules are focused around completion dates, which for the procrastinator is no use at all.

Once you discover the joy of completing tasks in good time or on time, your belief in yourself will slowly change—and you will have time to be happy on your own terms, too.

THIS WEEK... Make a start

Look around your home or your place of work, and make a list of all the things that you have started, but not finished. If you feel yourself procrastinating at the very thought of starting, just write down one thing. If you are serious in your quest for happiness, choose to do this now.

- Next, think about when you would like (or when you need) to have completed this task. Circle the date on your schedule.

- Work backward in your mind through the various tasks and stages that you will need to complete in order to achieve your end goal. Think about this in stages, according to the complexity of the task.

- Think of a realistic time span for each completion stage, and then repeat the exercise, doubling the amount of time you initially thought was necessary to complete each one.

- The chances are, if you have already been procrastinating, that the date you come up with was some days or weeks earlier than today's date, telling you that you should have started by now and you are behind already. Normally, you would panic at this point and choose to do something else, as a diversion. Instead, tell yourself that you now have three choices: to arrange to extend the deadline; to ask someone to help you to deliver on time; or both. Sticking your head in the sand and pretending that time is malleable is no longer an option—because it isn't.

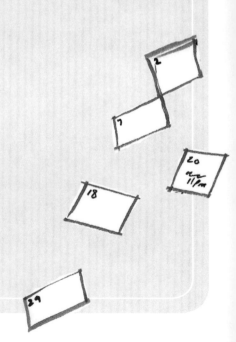

REFLECT... ON STOPPING PROCRASTINATION

_____

_____

_____

_____

_____

_____

_____

_____

_____

_____

_____

_____

_____

_____

_____

_____

_____

_____

_____

_____

SURROUND YOURSELF WITH POSITIVE PEOPLE

You may not realize that your happiness levels are being affected by the people you spend time with, so it's worth tuning in to how your mood is affected by the company of others. When you surround yourself with people who "fill your cup" rather than "drain it," you are much more likely to feel positive and happy.

For example, if you started the day feeling good and a phone call from a friend left you feeling deflated, ask yourself if this friend always makes you feel this way. Conversely, if a night out with someone left you feeling happy and full of energy, was it because that person has a "can-do" approach to life? Do you always feel this good after spending time with him or her? At work are there colleagues who are always encouraging and productive, whatever the challenges? It makes sense that they will have a more positive effect on your well-being and success at work than those who complain all the time. We can't necessarily rid ourselves of negative people (they may be those closest to us!), but we can be aware of how they affect us. You can also become one of the positive people in their life and fill their cup with a little happiness.

THIS WEEK... Enjoy some positive people power

Tune into the positive people in your life and why they are good for you.

- Think of three people whose company you really enjoy.
- Now consider the effect they usually have on you. Are they supportive, complimentary, energized, nurturing?
- Think about their positive behavior and what you like about their approach and attitude. Are there aspects that you could introduce into your own life this week?

REFLECT... ON BEING AROUND POSITIVE PEOPLE

_____
_____
_____
_____
_____
_____
_____
_____
_____
_____
_____
_____
_____
_____
_____
_____
_____
_____
_____
_____

LEARN TO FORGIVE

Anger, rage, and resentment can be all-consuming. They are strong emotions that can take over the body, both physically and mentally. It is natural to feel irritated and angry from time to time, but the irony is that if we hold on to anger, or the feelings get out of control, it will wreak more damage upon us than the person or situation we are angry with.

When someone becomes angry, their blood pressure rises, their heart rate increases, and they may be moved either to tears of frustration or a burst of temper. When we are happy, there is a similar physical reaction—but the outcome is joy and laughter instead of temper. It is very difficult to feel anger and happiness at the same time.

The most effective weapon against anger is often humor because it has the power to alter one state of mind to another. That's why the child who is bullied in the playground so often becomes the clown, to get out of trouble; and why international diplomats often have the gift of wit and charm, to defuse difficult situations before they flare up.

Sometimes, of course, anger runs much deeper. It may be the result of suffering emotional pain or hurt; you may have been storing up grudges over a long period of time. It may become a deeply held rage that you don't want to let go of. Over time it becomes a part of who you are and may lead you toward feelings of depression. Denying it will drive it deeper, so that it comes out inappropriately at other times. It is hard to feel happy when you are carrying such a load.

THE POWER OF FORGIVENESS

The antidote to deeply held anger is forgiveness. It is the decision to let go of feelings of resentment, the choice to forgive the person who has hurt you—not necessarily to condone what they have done, although responsibility often rests with both sides, but to set yourself free from the grasp of the anger. It is not an easy thing to do. The other person may not be ready to change.

Some victims of violent crime describe having to repeat this process of forgiveness regularly, as the memories return and the feelings rise again. Those who succeed in finding it within themselves to forgive, say that they now have a chance of happiness again. With forgiveness comes a sense of peace and the sense that you can continue with your life. It means committing to a process of change.

THIS WEEK... Challenge your anger

Ask yourself the following:

- "Why am I hanging on to my anger? What value is it to me?"
- "What would happen if I exchanged my anger for forgiveness? How would I feel within myself?"
- Consider how the situation to date has affected you and whether you have become a victim of your anger because it has become a part of who you are.
- Focus on thinking about the person who has caused you hurt, and if possible consider their side of the story.
- See whether you can find it within yourself to forgive the person, even if you can't forgive their words or their actions.

You may need to repeat this process more than once, but in shifting your attention to letting go of anger you will gradually become free of the situation that is stealing a part of your life and happiness.

REFLECT... ON FORGIVENESS

_____
_____
_____
_____
_____
_____
_____
_____
_____
_____
_____
_____
_____
_____
_____
_____
_____
_____
_____
_____

ESCAPE LONELINESS

Have you ever had the experience of suddenly realizing that someone you once knew hasn't been in touch for some time? How did you react? Did you feel rejected by their apparent lack of interest? Did you send them a text or pick up the phone? Or did you think, they can call me? All too often we take another's silence as personal rejection instead of stopping to consider what might be going on in their life.

Loneliness and happiness are rarely companions; when one appears, the other tends to leave the building. Humans are by nature social creatures. When we are feeling sad or lonely, other people's joy and laughter can feel like weapons, sent to mock our own sense of isolation from the world. On the other hand, rediscovering a sense of happiness can make loneliness feel like a thing of the past—almost instantly; our troubles seem more manageable; life feels worth living.

How does one state become the other; and how can a helping hand be offered to those who feel cut off from the world?

Many people are happy to spend time alone; it can be enriching to spend quiet time in thought or contemplation, or simply to feel free to enjoy personal space without interruption. Alone time and loneliness are totally different things. Being alone is a choice; whereas loneliness, like grief, feels more like being cut adrift.

The dark thud of loneliness can lead to terrible feelings of emptiness and isolation. It is painful, and for some people leads to problems with alcohol or drugs; it may lead to depression and a lack of self-care; it has triggered some people to violence. As hurdles go, loneliness may seem one of the highest, but in reality, it is less of a hurdle and more of a barrier—and an invisible one at that.

All too often the lonely person will push people away, sometimes with anger, and try not to register their concern, refusing any help, however well-meant. But there are steps away from loneliness that can be taken, if the person who is suffering is willing to give them a try.

Some people become lonely because they are grieving for the loss of a partner; others may feel cut off from old friends; or be too shy to feel confident in company, and believe they don't "fit in" with others. Some who are facing a difficult time in life may cut themselves off, not wanting their troubles to be a burden to others.

At the heart of someone's loneliness may be an inability to share emotions, or trust other people; beneath the outer shell may lie a lack of self-confidence or a sense of feeling unlovable. It can be hard to ask others for help when you are feeling so alone.

TAKING SMALL STEPS

You cannot walk toward happiness and loneliness at the same time. They live at opposite ends of the same road. The first step toward happiness involves taking a conscious step forward, without giving a backward glance.

- Take some time to focus on your feelings, to understand what is making you feel this way. Learning how to practice meditation can be immensely helpful.
- Taking up walking, running, or any form of mildly aerobic exercise can help to beat

THIS WEEK... Reach out

Do one thing that puts you in the company of other people.

- Accept invitations or offers of help.
- Go to places where you are likely to meet people, such as the park, library, or meet-up groups in your local area.
- Arrange to meet an old friend face-to-face, rather than communicating via phone or social media. You are much more likely to tell someone what is really going on if you spend proper time with them, have eye contact, and know they are listening to you.

If there aren't friends you can turn to, seek the help and advice of a healthcare professional, such as a doctor or nurse, or a counselor, knowing there will be 100 percent confidentiality. Be open about your true feelings and what is really going on in your life.

the blues. It will help to increase the levels of endorphins in your body, and give you a natural lift.

- Look at your behavior and lifestyle and how it might be adding to your own sense of isolation. Consider whether you need help with overeating, drinking, or other issues.
- Even when you are at home alone make an effort to take care of your appearance—it can make a difference to how you feel about yourself.
- Pay attention to small things in your life that give you pleasure—birdsong, color, a piece of music—and focus on their detail.
- A good laugh works wonders—do you have a favorite movie that is guaranteed to make you laugh?

REFLECT... ON ESCAPING LONELINESS AND REACHING OUT

_____

_____

_____

_____

_____

_____

_____

_____

_____

_____

_____

_____

_____

_____

_____

_____

_____

_____

_____

_____

_____

WE ARE ALL CONNECTED

Doris Pilkington (Nugi Garimara) was an award-winning Australian writer of Aboriginal descent, best known internationally for her book *Follow the Rabbit-Proof Fence*, which was turned into an excellent film. I attended one of her talks a few years ago and was struck by her opening lines. She told the audience that in Aboriginal culture, when you ask someone, "How are you today?" it is understood that you are enquiring not just about the person in front of you, but about their ancestors, too.

The question is taken very seriously, because well-being does not relate solely to an individual. It relates to all the people connected to them in their family and in their community, to their environment in its broadest sense, and to their past—because we are all connected and we have a shared history. The concept took my breath away.

When a question is asked with such sincerity, and the answer given with such perspective, it immediately has more meaning. "How. Are. You?" How can you ever ask the question lightly again?

Would everyone be happier if we all took the question more seriously; if we asked it in a way that tuned into people's true state of mind? Those who reply with a half-hearted, "I'm fine," are more often than not saying, "Actually, I'm not fine. I'm not too happy really and I would love it if someone had time to chat to me a while."

If someone is unhappy, it is a reflection on those around them. Something is out of balance. In speaking to an unhappy person, you have a chance to influence their mood and make them feel connected once again. If the gift of listening is given to one person, they are more likely to pass it on to another.

The person who feels listened to, cared for, and supported is much more likely to reply, "I'm very well, thank you; great, actually," which allows you to say, "That's wonderful. I'm so glad—please tell me what's been happening in your life."

DEAL WITH NEGATIVE FEELINGS

Jealousy and envy are the enemies of happiness because they focus on the things we feel are missing in our lives—often the things over which we have no control. When we compare ourselves with others, we find ourselves wanting (literally). As Othello learned to his cost in Shakespeare's play, jealousy has the power to destroy lives, and takes away the happiness of the one who is consumed by jealous imaginings.

Learning how to deal with jealousy and envy when they strike can make the difference between living a life with full and joyous heart, and carrying around a heavy heart that is angry and shriveling. That sounds melodramatic—but for many people the impact is dramatic.

Envy is the result of wanting what someone else has, or comparing your situation with another person's and finding something wanting in your own circumstances. It can happen at any stage in life and can hit quite suddenly. Jealousy is the emotional response to someone else having what you feel is rightly yours. It is one of the oddities of being human that, as adults, we can feel completely content with our lives until suddenly confronted with someone who has made different life choices and who has what we envisaged for ourselves. We may think we have left sibling rivalry in our childhood, but it has a habit of raising its head throughout life. We know we love our friends, but sometimes the differences in your lives makes it hard to relate to one another as you used to. Some common scenarios that lead to envy and jealousy are:

- You bump into an old boyfriend or girlfriend and immediately dislike his or her new partner for no real reason.
- You have been looking forward to seeing your sibling, but pick a fight over a petty detail to divert from your envy that he or she can afford a wonderful vacation.
- You are looking forward to a reunion with former colleagues, but leave the evening deflated because their lives seem to be more successful than your own.

- You feel angry with yourself for feeling so jealous instead of happy when your best friend announces she is pregnant—because you badly want children of your own.
- You are close to your siblings, but fall out with them over care arrangements for your elderly parent. You think you know better than they do what he or she might have wanted.

THE CHOICE IS YOURS

Happiness begins from within. Others cannot give us happiness, and nor can they take it away. It is impossible to feel truly happy and fulfilled while we are jealous or thinking ill of others. In undermining their contentment, we diminish our own.

We choose our own responses to the opportunities we are given; we can also choose whether to hold on to negative feelings that are not helping us to live to the full or let them go. To echo the words of St Francis of Assisi, joy arises from accepting the things we cannot change and finding it within ourselves to change the things we can. There will always be people who appear to have more than we do. We can only wish others as much happiness as we would like for ourselves.

Week 16

RELEASING NEGATIVE FEELINGS

A momentary pang of discontent can be a motivator; it might awaken the competitive part of you that shouts, "I want that; I can do that, too." If it spurs you into action to bring about a change that you definitely want, the impact can be very positive. But if comparisons leave you feeling angry or sorry for yourself, there are a few other solutions to try:

- Pay attention to your body. Notice how you are feeling, and which areas of your body are being most affected. Are you feeling angry, tense, sad, frightened? Are you feeling the sensation in your stomach, your shoulders, your jaw, your heart?
- Take a deep breath and move your body. Shake your arms; jump on the spot; force yourself to smile; go for a run; find somewhere to shout in private, or to cry.
- Do something physical to shift the tension and encourage yourself to relax. (Reaching for a drink, the chocolate, or ramping up the speed while you go for a drive, are not such constructive reactions.)
- Many people find exercise or meditation to be useful—to release physical tension and help focus your mind on what truly has meaning in your life.

THIS WEEK... Make time for self-reflection

Consider the following:
- The choices that you would have had to make to achieve what you are coveting. Do you regret having made alternative decisions? Can you find it within yourself to forgive yourself and move on?
- The life or situation you have now. What is it that you are dissatisfied with? What steps can you take to change things? When will you begin?
- The aspects of your life or situation that make you happy. What would you not be without? Give yourself space to reflect on these and be thankful that you are blessed.

REFLECT... ON DEALING WITH NEGATIVE FEELINGS

_____

_____

_____

_____

_____

_____

_____

_____

_____

_____

_____

_____

_____

_____

_____

_____

_____

_____

_____

BE MORE CURIOUS

It is hard to be truly happy when we think we know it all. Knowing it all shuts the door on new experiences. Enthusiasm and excitement, on the other hand, are spurred by anticipation of the unknown. As we grow older, our tendency is to become jaded by novelty. We may forget that life can be fun; we think we have seen it all before. We judge new experiences by the things we have already seen and done, but in doing so we potentially close our minds to enjoying life or seeing things in a new way. Our sense of enthusiasm becomes dulled around the edges. Not only do we stop learning new things, we also start to forget the things we already know.

We can learn a lot from children and animals. Children love the joy of new things. The anticipation of a fun day out can be all-consuming. They are endlessly curious about what other people are doing and saying, and how other children are playing; but they can become bored just as quickly, once familiarity has killed the novelty. The excitement of something new makes children active, bouncy, and happy, and hungry to know more; the disappointment of boredom a little later makes them slump, cry, or become still.

Have you ever noticed an animal's reaction when something new is brought into their environment? Their first impulse is to sniff it, pounce on it, chew it, or otherwise explore it, in an attempt to conquer it and make it their own. Even the most elderly cat will muster up the whiskers to check out a new arrival or test the limits of a new object. Just watching the ritual can be amusing but it is interesting, too, to see how alive the animal becomes as it adjusts its perception and learns something new about its world.

Curiosity stimulates the brain and feeds creativity; new experiences keep us feeling young at heart and lively in spirit. Think of people you know who are creative, and chances

are they like to mix things up a little. They might be a bit disordered and impulsive, but life just seems a bit more fun when they are around. The people who have retained their sense of curiosity are the comedians, musicians, artists, writers, and others among us who bring spontaneous joy and laughter into our world.

CHECK YOUR ATTITUDE

Here are a few warning signs that you might be getting a little set in your ways—and some ideas for resetting the dial to youthful curiosity:

- When did you last go out of your way to watch a firework display? If it was cold, did you brave the weather and feel a sense of excitement, or did you watch from indoors, or turn away?
- What is your reaction to major snowfall? Do you think of it as an obstacle to be cleared or as a winter playground—for you, as well as the kids?
- What is the age range of your friends and acquaintances? Are most of them of the same generation as you?
- When did you last learn something new?

THIS WEEK... Do something different

Happiness thrives on variety and fun. Resist the temptation to keep everything the same and this week push yourself out of your comfort zone.

- Change one or two aspects of your routine.
- Take up a new activity (see Week 38 for more ideas).
- Make an effort to interact with new people outside of your usual circle.
- Try cooking something different to your usual meals or head out to a new restaurant.
- Change the channel on the TV and watch a different type of program to usual.

Week 17

REFLECT... ON BEING MORE CURIOUS

APPRECIATE YOUR UNIQUENESS

Everything you need to be happy today or in the future lies within you right now. Wishing you were someone else with other talents and skills, or regretting that you did or didn't make a certain decision, will take you further away from happiness. Looking yourself in the eye and appreciating who you are with all your beauty, skills, and potential, will take you to wherever you have the determination to be.

Who could fail to be inspired by athletes in not only the Olympics, but especially the Paralympics? Athletes overcome a range of physical and mental challenges to come together from all over the world to compete with others who are the best in the world. The Paralympics shows us all that disabilities that would challenge many to remain positive are no barrier to success—tenacity, focus, training, guts, and skill gave each person a unique opportunity to succeed.

At the University of Pennsylvania in the USA, leading psychologist Dr Martin Seligman and colleagues are compiling an ongoing study into the factors that create authentic happiness. Online questionnaires can be completed by anyone who registers online.

Seligman has found that one of the most important conditions of happiness is having strong awareness and appreciation of our own talents. When we understand what we are good at, we become more confident in our competence and happier in ourselves.

Appreciating your uniqueness requires you to pay as much attention to yourself as you would to other people; it means listening to the complimentary things that people might say and believing that there is merit in them. It also means absorbing criticism, no matter how hard it is to hear, and realizing that there are things about yourself that you might choose to improve or change.

WHO ARE YOU?

You are a unique combination of the personal traits, physical and mental skills, attitudes and abilities that make you who you are. By recognizing and celebrating these, you will be better able to channel your attention in a direction that will be fulfilling, and also make you happy.

- How would you describe yourself in a single sentence?
- Do you describe yourself according to your role at work? As a parent? Or as an individual with unique talents?
- What are your strongest personality traits? For example, would you call yourself trustworthy? Loyal? Strong? Determined? Hardworking? Kind? Fair? Tolerant? Brave?
- Give yourself a minute to write down all the words you associate with yourself, and then divide them into positive and negative.
- Consider the negative list and reframe each word in a way that shows it to be a positive skill in some circumstances.

THIS WEEK... Create a happiness resume

This resume (CV) focuses on your personal path but can include work as part of your achievements.

- Write down your list of achievements, as far back as you can remember. Organize it by date and by year. Include vacations you have arranged, events shared with friends, things you have enjoyed doing on your own, with children, your partner, your pets. Include your work achievements, if you like. Wherever you have been and whatever you have done in your life that has made you happy, proud, or respected—capture it on paper.
- Look at the list again. What skills, interests, outlook, or passions are central to your resume? What are the themes that continue to appear? Being sociable? Enjoying art, music, theater, sport? Studying? Gardening? Making people feel safe and nurtured?

You may find this process stays with you for some time. New things will come to mind and provide another brushstroke for the picture.

REFLECT... ON APPRECIATING YOUR UNIQUENESS

THINK LIKE A LOTTERY WINNER

If you were to win the lottery tomorrow, how would you feel? What would you do to celebrate? Would you invest your winnings, share them, spend them? After the initial euphoria passed, what do you think you would value the most about your home, your friends, your family—and the world? Would anything have changed in your life?

The lottery mentality is interesting because it encourages us to think in extremes. By pushing the limits of our imagination we tap into another part of ourselves that tends to be restrained by daily commitments, habits of thought, and financial circumstances. It may not be possible to improve the material side of your life overnight—but you don't need to wait until you win the lottery to start becoming the person you would ideally like to be.

When people are asked which would make them happier, winning the lottery or spending life confined to a wheelchair, the vast majority will choose the lottery win—and in the short term they would be correct. In a scientifically controlled study, however, it was found that neither change makes a fundamental difference to people's levels of happiness in the longer term. Six months after winning the lottery or being wheelchair-bound, both groups of people were equally happy. Happiness is not something that happens *to* us, it comes from within.

THIS WEEK... Develop a winning mentality

Try asking yourself:
- What are you putting off doing until the conditions are right, that you could start doing right now?
- What could you do for someone else that would make them feel as if it was their lucky day?
- In what ways are you already a lottery winner?
- What are the keys to unlocking your more adventurous side?

REFLECT... ON THINKING LIKE A LOTTERY WINNER

_____

_____

_____

_____

_____

_____

_____

_____

_____

_____

_____

_____

_____

_____

_____

_____

_____

_____

_____

DISCOVER THE ART OF GIVING

There is a secret to giving that not everyone has discovered but which is a source of optimism for the world. The good news is that giving to others is good for you. It will make you happy. It will make you feel better about yourself.

I spoke recently to someone whose mother had moved to a smaller home. Sorting through all her possessions and deciding what to let go had been painful for both of them. Even passing books and goods on to a thrift store had proved a hard adjustment. But the charity they chose runs a scheme whereby donors are sent an update on how much money their items have raised. Receiving these letters made my friend's mother so happy that over time she began to give away even more.

In 2010, the Charities Aid Foundation (CAF) joined with *The Sunday Times* to ask 69 of the UK's wealthiest people about the reasons for their philanthropy. The majority said the main reason was that they enjoyed giving. Over half wanted to leave a positive legacy. In the United States, Bill Gates is leading the way via the Bill and Melinda Gates Foundation. He has personally donated millions of dollars and, with Warren Buffett, has launched "The Giving Pledge," inviting billionaires to make a moral pledge to leave at least 50 percent of their fortunes as a legacy to philanthropic causes. Media mogul Simon Cowell has been quoted in the past as crediting Oprah Winfrey for helping him to discover how surprisingly good it feels to give money away.

SERVING OTHERS

But giving isn't just about money. The most valuable gift of all is your personal time —time spent in the service of others, listening and paying attention. The concept of service may seem old-fashioned in the modern world, but the nature of service goes much deeper than the odd good deed. When we are able to serve others, modestly, but putting the needs of the ego to one side, we become more humble, less focused on self, and more aware of the strengths of those around us.

We can also give by simply being kind to others. Studies have proven again and again that the quickest and most satisfying route to finding happiness is not to think about yourself all the time, but instead to focus on other people and what they need. As human beings we are social creatures who like to be connected to one another. Giving and gratitude are essential ingredients in the formulation and experience of happiness.

Finally, think of others' happiness before your own. If everyone's mission on this earth was to help others to become happy first, what an incentive that would be to speed up the process. If none of us could be happy until everyone else was happy, what would we do first to increase happiness for the greatest number of people?

THIS WEEK... Pledge to be good

Try taking the Good Deed Pledge. It may turn out to be the best good deed you have ever done for yourself!

- Consider pledging to yourself and others today that you will consciously do one good deed per day, no matter how small, for the next ten days; and that, at the end of those ten days, you will repeat the pledge.
- Make a list of deeds done and ask yourself whether or not each one made you happy.
- You may also enjoy subscribing to the Kindness Calendar (see page 189).

REFLECT... ON THE ART OF GIVING

BE STILL AND CALM

Finding your way to a place of calm inside your mind is to find a place where transformation can occur and peace can be found. This is the role of prayer and meditation and much of the function of spiritual rituals. The aim is to change your state of mind from a place of busy-ness to one of stillness and contemplation.

Some people find a more active route to calm, via yoga, tai chi, chanting, or running. I find my own path to stillness by walking through the countryside or city in the cool of the morning, although those with greater wisdom than me tell me that this is not the same as sitting still and allowing your thoughts to find their own way to resolution.

We all need periods of calm and quiet order. In those moments when we are simply still, transition takes place and things become clearer in our minds.

For some, meditation is the way to stillness. Finding your own route within yourself will take time and practice. It is a skill I have yet to master, but what I do know is how clearly it has transformed the lives of other people, and the tangible benefits they find it provides.

Ella, a writer and speaker, finds meditation helps her to focus, brings new ideas into her mind, and gives her a greater depth of understanding in her work. Sue, a PR consultant, says her meditation practice provides her with a period of deep calm amid the pace and pressure of each day. It reduces her blood pressure and puts her back in touch with herself. Rick, a businessman, makes a conscious effort to set aside time for meditation practice each day. On the days when it is not possible, he finds he is less able to control his feelings of annoyance; he is less focused and feels less grounded. Meditation is a vital part of his commitment to inviting peace and happiness into his life.

THIS WEEK... Just breathe

At its simplest level, finding a route to calm is about breathing. Choose a place where there is no likelihood of interruption or distractions and that is neither too hot nor too cold.

- Lie down on your back on the floor.
- Let your feet flop outward and relax your hands so that your palms, facing up, and fingers find their own natural position.
- Close your eyes and relax your mind.
- Don't worry about where your thoughts are taking you. Don't focus on them. Just let them come and go as they please.
- Focus on your breath.
- Breathe in deeply; and then breathe out fully; breathe in fully and breathe out fully.
- Let your breath find its own rhythm, but keep the breaths deep.
- Maintain this for as long as you feel comfortable.
- Focus only on your breath.

You may find that when you first try to do this, you fall asleep. You may find, too, that your breath is coming from your upper body instead of your lower diaphragm and that you are holding your breath instead of letting it flow. Try to practice breathing with your hand on your belly. It should inflate with the in-breath and deflate with the out-breath. It will come with practice.

REFLECT... ON BEING STILL AND CALM

SEE THE FUNNY SIDE OF LIFE

Happiness and laughter are the Fred Astaire and Ginger Rogers of contentment. Where laughter leads, happiness follows (although not necessarily backward, or in high heels). Genuine laughter transforms the body's energy. Someone who is convulsed with laughter literally shakes. Belly laughs are called belly laughs for a reason—they come from deep within the body and are a release of energy.

Of course, not all laughter is a force for good. Some laughter is mocking or dark. Laughter is very close to tears sometimes. Those who work in the medical world will often develop a macabre sense of humor to protect themselves from the emotional impact of the tragedies they see each day. We laugh when our hearts are breaking because we don't dare to give in to the feelings that will take over if we don't. But in the course of finding happiness, laughter is about letting go of the dark side and finding our way to the light and joy of each day.

Lorna was a talented artist, but by the time I met her, when she was in her late eighties, she was hampered by poor eyesight and arthritis, so was no longer able to paint or walk unassisted. However, she loved the natural world and with her artist's eye for observation and detail she was still inspired and entertained by what she could see—both in her mind's eye and in reality. Her greatest pleasure was to sit by the window and watch the birds forage for food and go about their daily rituals. She recognized each one and gave them names, and was constantly amused by their antics. I would be told hilarious tales of the latest happenings in the bird world each time I visited her.

As she often used to say, it was her sense of the absurd that made life enjoyable. Without her ability to look on the funny side of life, her older age would have been far more painful.

HOW MANY WAYS HAVE YOU LAUGHED LATELY?

According to journalist Nick Harding, the 40 million speakers of Marathi in India use at least eight different words to describe laughter:

- *Khudukhudu*: The soft giggles of a young child
- *Phidiphid*: Raucous laughter
- *Hyahya*: Polite laughter
- *Khadakhada*: Children laughing loudly
- *Khaskhas*: Mild chuckles
- *Khokho*: Laughter that is loud and rowdy
- *Khikhi*: Laughing like a horse
- *Phisphis*: Mocking or disparaging laughter

CHECK YOUR LAUGHTER METER

Do you remember what it feels like to be overcome with giggles or shake with uncontrollable laughter so that it was impossible to speak? To feel consumed by the joy of a single moment, shared with someone you care about or can have fun with? It probably happened frequently when you were growing up, but as we get older it becomes less common for us to let go and have a really good laugh.

Laughter wipes away tension in a single breath and turns a frowning face into one that is alive and beautiful. It doesn't take much to trigger a giggle: just thinking about something funny that has happened in the past can provoke laughter and increase happiness. When we are tense, we become very serious—but turning things around in your mind can be a great way to change your mood and find the lighter side of life.

- Check your laughter meter. When is the last time you had a really great laugh? Do you know what makes you laugh?

- When was the last time you laughed at yourself? When was the last time someone else had a laugh at your expense, without you taking it personally? Is there a chance you take yourself too seriously? Do you need to lighten up a bit in order to enjoy life?

THIS WEEK... Have a giggle

Make a conscious effort to have a sense of humor this week. Find something to laugh about every day if you can.

- Most of us know someone who makes us laugh and with whom we can really let our hair down. Make time to meet up with or connect with him or her. Recalling old times and chuckling about new ones is a wonderful shortcut to happiness.

- Consider treating yourself to a self-styled comedy night. Hire the funniest film you can find and allow yourself to remember what it feels like to laugh just for the sake of it.

- Tell a silly joke, read a favorite cartoon strip, look for the absurd in every situation.

REFLECT... ON SEEING THE FUNNY SIDE OF LIFE

DO SOMETHING CREATIVE

Life can often get in the way of doing the things we really love. While you may not have the freedom to use your creativity in your day-to-day work, making a space for it in your life will enhance your happiness.

Like many people, you may spend time dreaming about something you love to do, perhaps an activity you used to do when you were younger, but constantly put it off because there just isn't time. It may be playing a musical instrument, baking, drawing or painting, for example. Or perhaps you want to take up a new creative activity, such as writing a blog or learning to dance. Now is the time to stop thinking and start doing!

REASONS TO BE CREATIVE

- Tapping into something creative will have a positive effect on your whole life, helping you to approach the more mundane activities in life more creatively too.
- Creative activities are rewarding and will make you feel more fulfilled, and the results may inspire those around you, too.
- Concentrating on a creative activity makes you focused and mindful, which is in itself relaxing. For that time at least, you won't be multi-tasking or running through your usual list of worries.

THIS WEEK... Create one thing!

Take action toward your first creative task.

- Plan time into your week to begin your creative task. This may involve getting up earlier or going to bed later but make the time to begin.
- Take action toward your goal, such as researching lessons or buying equipment.

- Ensure that the time you set aside will not be interrupted. Make it clear to those who rely on you that you aren't available.
- Tell a friend or loved one what you are planning to do. You may be more likely to stick to your creative goal if someone else knows about it and encourages you.

REFLECT... ON CREATIVITY

_____

_____

_____

_____

_____

_____

_____

_____

_____

_____

_____

_____

_____

_____

_____

_____

_____

_____

_____

_____

TAKE A RISK

Have you the courage to let go of the person you think you are right now in order to find happiness? Are you brave enough to live life to the full? For most of our lives, we may choose to live within a personal comfort zone of familiarity and safety; in doing so we think we remain safe from harm and away from failure. But the truth is that the safer we feel, the more afraid we become, because doing something unfamiliar feels increasingly daunting. A very safe life can become an anxious life, lived within self-limiting boundaries.

Happiness may become unhappiness because we are not living a life that is fulfilled. Interestingly, it is when we risk failure that we learn the most; and it is when we start to stretch ourselves that our potential for happiness increases.

WHAT ROLE DO YOU PLAY?

Sometimes we are so attached to a particular view of ourselves that we don't realize that it is holding us back. What words do you use to describe yourself? Are you the shy one, the sporty one, the clever one, the one who is hopeless at x, y, or z? Where do the origins of those beliefs come from? Are they really true? What opportunities are you not taking because you can't see yourself in the role? How does it feel to try on some other labels for size, such as, I have courage, I have talent, I have the tenacity to succeed, I am a dancer, I am a singer, I am good at sport, I am an attractive person, I am sociable, I am happy. The brain appreciates clear direction and will fulfill your new instructions if you keep repeating them over a period of time.

There are several different kinds of happiness, but the hardest won are those moments resulting from an extreme of effort, where we have learned something new, achieved a long-term goal, have done battle with ourselves or our environment—and won. Doing your best and achieving the outcome you hoped for reaps long-term rewards. It is a state of happiness well earned and well deserved.

FEEL THE FEAR...

Susan Jeffers' bestselling self-help book *Feel the Fear and Do It Anyway* gives people the tools to move beyond a place of procrastination, indecision, and fear and take action. This might range from something like facing up to a fear of public speaking to having the courage to leave an unhappy relationship and deal with the emotional and practical consequences that brings. When we address our fears and move beyond them, we become empowered, we grow as a person, and this ultimately leads to us feeling happier in ourselves.

THIS WEEK... Change your attitude to risk

Do you embrace new situations fully and worry about the consequences afterward; or do you choose not to try because you don't want to risk failure? Whatever your attitude, decide on a new challenge and choose to behave in a way that is opposite to your usual behavior.

- If you are risk averse, just say yes to the opportunity; you may discover that you are better at thinking on your feet than you realized.

- If you usually leap before thinking, decide this time to ask advice or create a plan. You may discover that when fully prepared, you can achieve even greater heights.

REFLECT... ON TAKING A RISK

NURTURE YOUR FRIENDSHIPS

According to scientific studies, teenagers show greater levels of self-esteem, personal motivation, strength of character, and levels of happiness when they are with their friends than in any other situation. It doesn't take a research project to figure that out, you may think—but interestingly, the same applies to adults. When adults spend periods of time with friends, they become more intensely happy than when they are with their partner, spouse, or children.

Friends are a vitally important ingredient for happiness. They bear witness to our lives and tell us stories of our own past. They help us to form and fulfill our dreams. They laugh with us, comfort us, and party with us—and they give us a boost when we're feeling low. Friends are part of our story and our journey. They remind us of who we are when we have lost our way.

But friendships, like gardens, need to be tended and cared for in order to grow. They can be all too easily squandered through inadvertent neglect, especially as we get older and allow the routine of life or the needs of our families to get in the way.

HOW TO BE A FRIEND

What makes you a good friend? When you think of yourself in relation to your friends, do you like what you see? Are you the kind of person who always provides a listening ear? Are you a leader who makes things happen? Are you the nurturer who always soothes the way? What could you do more of that would make people happier? What could you do less of that would make someone's day?

VIRTUAL FRIENDSHIPS

We live in an age where it's easy to maintain contact through social media, but without ever properly communicating. We may have hundreds of so-called friends, but not even have a phone number or postal address for most of them. Ironically, we may spend more time finding out about the lives of people on social media whom we are not that close to, at the expense of spending quality time with our real friends.

    We can satisfy ourselves that we're staying in touch with a friend because we read their regular posts and look at their photos, but in fact we only know about their virtual life. We know all about the events they choose to share, but nothing of their real everyday issues. Commenting on each other's news or posting some news of your own is not enough for a friendship to flourish. Speaking, writing, or seeing each other will have far more impact.

THIS WEEK... Make a round table of friendship

Whose friendship do you value in your life and why? Who would you turn to in a crisis—or to have a great time?

- Think of your circle of friends as King Arthur's knights of the round table: who would be sitting around the table with you, and why?

- When you bring each friend to mind, ask yourself why you value that person, and whether you have done enough to show how much he or she means to you.
- Do your friends know that you value them highly? Perhaps it's time you told them.

REFLECT... ON NURTURING YOUR FRIENDSHIPS

THE RELATIONSHIP DANCE

The quest for love and happiness is universal. It begins in babyhood, where the close bond formed between baby and mother is instinctive, overwhelming, and based on survival. The kind of loving we have as young children influences the way our brain is wired and helps to form our character; it has an impact on our teenage and adult choices, when the search for a loving relationship begins.

There is a romantic myth that tells us relationships are built on "happy ever after," but the reality is rather more complicated, and potentially more rewarding. Human beings are not fixed in their development; they are forever changing. So whatever form your relationship takes will change constantly.

Love in its early stages is often about looking for points of similarity and connection; personal differences are overlooked or modified or tolerated; communication is intense and constant; happiness is easily won in exchange for a look or a kiss; the couple are

looking for reasons to spend more time together rather than push each other away. Such intensity of feeling is hard to sustain unchallenged. At some point, the rhythm changes and real life comes into play, and then choices and compromises have to be made.

LEARNING THE STEPS

Are you paying attention? Are you paying your partner enough attention, or do you take each other for granted? Are you truly communicating with each other, or are you just passing the time of day? Pressure at work may mean that office demands take over; the challenge of raising children and running a home may take their toll; the passionate intensity of the relationship may shift, leaving a couple wondering whether their connection was built on physical attraction rather than love, after all. Where are your priorities? Ask yourself, what are you willing to do to help things to change? Do you think "we" or "me"? Ask many people what they mean by happiness and they will describe things that provide them with calm, serenity, a sense of euphoria, or a feeling of belonging. Achieving this state in a relationship takes time. The difference between building a relationship and living parallel lives lies in the willingness to respect each other's needs, and finding the ground where mutual agreement can be found.

When you have a disagreement, does love win the day, or does your hurt pride put up a wall of resistance? Do you think in terms of "my needs versus your needs" or is your focus more on "our mutual needs"? For those who learn to dance in step and with good heart, a loving relationship can be ever more rewarding.

Are you ready to be happy? Seeking love may begin as a search for perfection. To be happy with who you have found usually requires a bit of adjustment and compromise. Ask yourself what you most love about the person you are with. What are you ready to build together? Can you appreciate each other's strengths and differences? Do you share similar goals? Do you share values? Are the two of you together greater than the two of you apart? Be honest with yourself—and stay in rhythm with the call of your heart.

SPEND TIME WITH ANIMALS!

There's a reason why two-thirds of US households have at least one pet—spending time with animals makes us happier and it can improve our health too.

According to research, when we stroke a furry animal for a few minutes it signals our brain to produce the calming chemicals serotonin and oxytocin, as well as decreasing the levels of cortisol, the stress hormone. A study in the *International Journal of Workplace Health Management* found that when people had access to a dog in the workplace, it had a calming influence and reduced stress levels.

PHYSICAL AND MENTAL HEALTH

Here are just some of the other reasons why owning a pet is good for you:

- Being responsible for an animal adds purpose and structure to the day.
- Caring for a pet makes us more caring, compassionate, and tolerant—all qualities that make us feel good about ourselves.
- Walking a dog regularly, or cleaning out a rabbit's hutch, means owners spend more time outdoors and are physically active, two things that increase happiness levels.
- Having a pet can stave off loneliness and be an ice-breaker for those who may struggle to socialize.

THIS WEEK... Hang out with animals

Find a way to be more animal-friendly:

- If you have a pet already, spend more time with it.
- If you don't have a pet, visit a friend who does—perhaps offer to walk a friend or neighbor's dog.
- If you really don't like getting up close and personal with animals, watch some cute animal videos—the internet is packed with them and they are bound to make you smile!

REFLECT... ON SPENDING TIME WITH ANIMALS

_____
_____
_____
_____
_____
_____
_____
_____
_____
_____
_____
_____
_____
_____
_____
_____

REFLECT... ON THE PAST SIX MONTHS

Now we're halfway through the year, how do you feel so far? What experiences
have made you feel joyful? In what ways are you content?

_____

_____

_____

_____

_____

_____

_____

_____

_____

_____

_____

_____

_____

_____

_____

_____

_____

_____

TAKE PRIDE IN YOUR APPEARANCE

Being vain is unlikely to make you happy because you'll become too focused on how you look. However, taking care of your appearance will improve how you feel about yourself, improving your confidence and sense of well-being.

We all love the occasional duvet day, but not getting dressed will affect your mood and your productivity. If you're feeling sluggish and a bit down in the dumps, having a shower, brushing your hair, and making an effort with what you wear is going to make you feel a whole lot better. People who work from home report being more productive if they get up and get dressed as if going into the office, than if they crawl from their bed to their desk in their sweatpants. Always assume someone might visit or that you might bump into someone you know when you go out.

TREAT YOURSELF!

You might feel that buying beauty products and new clothes is wasteful, but a simple purchase can also boost your self-esteem. Giving something back to yourself is okay, especially when you work hard and spend time caring for others. If you are a parent, you are sending a positive message about self-care and self-worth to your children, too. On a low budget? A regular haircut or a range of accessories can add a fresh lift to well-loved attire.

THIS WEEK... Declutter your wardrobe

When did you last overhaul your wardrobe? Now is the time!

- Throw out any clothes that are too tight or need repair. Wearing them is never going to make you feel good.

- If you haven't worn an item of clothing in the past 12 months, you probably never will. Throw it out or give it away.
- From the items you keep, put together proper outfits. Work out which items you could do with adding or replacing.

REFLECT... ON TAKING PRIDE IN YOUR APPEARANCE

PUT YOURSELF IN ANOTHER'S SHOES

Seeing the world through another's eyes lies at the heart of our capacity for kindness, community, kinship, and ultimately, happiness. Unless we can feel compassion for other people's troubles and unless we can try to appreciate what it must feel like to see things from other perspectives, we are simply islands—separated from one another by our indifference and selfishness.

Empathy is the capacity to understand the world from another's point of view. It is not about feeling sorry for someone or judging them; it is the ability to realize, "I have my opinion, but I can appreciate why you might see the situation differently." Empathy is quite a sophisticated skill. We are not born with it. The frontal lobes of the brain are the area that helps us to develop reasoning skills, take responsibility, and apply our intelligence. They begin to develop at about two years old, which is also when we start to understand that not everyone sees the world the same way we do. The brain develops the capacity for empathy over time as we learn to share, take turns, forgive,

and appreciate each other's differences. Empathy turns our focus outward instead of inward and helps us to be more understanding.

There are times when being empathetic is challenging. If another driver were to run into your car, it might be hard to choose to see things from their point of view, but getting into a battle of words wouldn't resolve the situation any more quickly. In fact, it may make it worse. Try to look forward to a point where you can forgive their misjudgment; try to use empathy to let go of your anger, so that even if the car was badly damaged, the lasting impact would be on the vehicle, not on you.

HOW EMPATHY HELPS US TO FIND HAPPINESS

When we tune into other people's moods, they affect our own sense of well-being, too. Just as we can be affected by someone else's sadness, so too we can pick up on his or her feelings of happiness. When we are able to make other people feel happy, some of it rubs off on us. That explains why we tend to enjoy the company of upbeat, happy people. Who do you know who makes others feel happy to be around them? Listen to their choice of language; hear how they talk to other people. Are they using humor? Do they tend to frame things in a positive way and give credit where credit is due?

THIS WEEK... Suspend judgment

Is there someone in your life whose attitude drives you crazy? Does someone close to you irritate you with some of their habits and points of view?

- Try to suspend your judgment of them for a while and put yourself in their shoes.

- Why do you think they feel the need to be this way? Is it simply a defense mechanism?
- What does your irritation say about you? Is there something about your attitude that you need to change?

REFLECT... ON PUTTING YOURSELF IN ANOTHER'S SHOES

DISCOVER LOVING KINDNESS

When we are young children, our own needs are all-consuming. Our focus is on our own comfort and survival; all else is secondary. As we grow older and our minds open and develop, we come to understand that the needs of other people are as important as our own. With this realization comes the richness of appreciating others and being appreciated ourselves; friendships grow; sacrifices are made for the greater good of a situation, and we discover that taking care of other people's needs reaps its own rewards. We feel loved, connected, of value, and appreciated; and it can make us feel good about ourselves, too. Happiness grows with loving kindness.

The concept of loving kindness lies at the heart of all faiths around the world. It focuses on paying loving attention to the needs of others—and loving them as ourselves. Loving kindness is not about selfless martyrdom but encourages us to use wise discernment in deciding how to act in any situation—with empathy, compassion, forgiveness, love, and understanding. In Buddhism it is known as Metta, in Sanskrit it is Maitreya. The Dalai Lama talks and writes about the steps toward loving kindness that are central to learning to follow a spiritual path.

OPENING UP

Each of us has the capacity for loving kindness, but sometimes it is consciously suppressed, due to an event that has happened in our lives. Perhaps a difficult decision taken at work has caused someone pain or hardship; perhaps a choice made in our personal life has had a negative impact on others; perhaps something so painful or hurtful has happened that we can't bear to look at it too closely. When life is tough, we toughen up to get through. Sometimes the walls of self-protection remain in place to prevent us from looking too closely at what has happened.

Loving kindness begins with forgiveness, in a way that allows you to make peace with yourself. No life is free of regrets. When we hang on to negative thoughts about ourselves, it becomes harder to act with love toward others, because the heart is closed and in pain.

THIS WEEK... Practice loving kindness

Sit or lie and relax into a meditative state (see page 145):

- Wish someone well whom you care about. Think of someone close to you. Consider the traits you appreciate about him or her; think of them with love and care; send them loving and kind thoughts and wish them well.

- Wish someone well whom you don't know. Think of someone who is familiar to you, but whom you don't know personally. You have neither positive nor negative feelings about him or her. Send loving and kind thoughts to wish them well, either in your mind or out loud.

- Wish someone well whom you find difficult. Consider someone whom you find hard to be with, or who has aggrieved you in some way. Consider your feelings of anger or resentment. Acknowledge those feelings and let them change and go. Send this person loving and kind thoughts. Wish him or her well, and wish them happiness.

- Wish loving kindness upon the world. Draw together in your mind these three people and yourself. Wish each of them well and extend loving kindness to the greater Universe. Try to spread your intention equally, without favoring one person more than another. Acknowledge that we are all connected, and that by offering loving kindness to one person, it can be extended to the world.

REFLECT... ON LOVING KINDNESS

_____

_____

_____

_____

_____

_____

_____

_____

_____

_____

_____

_____

_____

_____

_____

_____

_____

_____

_____

_____

_____

SPIRITUAL AWARENESS

Many people lose their sense of happiness because they come to believe their life has no meaning. There are as many reasons for this as there are people on the planet. To paraphrase Tolstoy, every lost person becomes lost in their own way. Does this sense of loss stem in part from an absence of spiritual influence in our lives? We are sentient as well as physical beings, and connect by using our senses and mind—but we are shy and often skeptical of the needs of the soul.

Scientists such as Martin Seligman, who have devoted their professional lives to understanding the nature of happiness, focus more on the mind than on the notion of soul, but they have discovered that those who succeed in living a purposeful life are the happiest.

A purposeful life tends to mean one that is focused on a goal or a mission that is greater than the needs of the individual alone. Altruism and selflessness enhance the chosen path. Great spiritual leaders, such as Mother Theresa, the Dalai Lama, and Archbishop Desmond Tutu, and more secular leaders, such as Nelson Mandela, Gandhi, and Aung San Suu Kyi, all display a calm hinterland and a sense of purpose that give them a spiritual quality. They are acting for the greater good; the quest to improve the well-being of others has overtaken any inclination to focus solely on their own needs.

For many, spiritual awareness involves a ritual of prayers, chants, hymns, and offerings of thanks. The vibration, rhythm, and symbolism of these ancient ways have a profound and uplifting effect on the human mind and body.

Many who seek spiritual awareness are seekers after the ultimate truths in life; they have faith in life's greater purpose or are searching for a state of bliss. Ironically, differences in spiritual doctrine and rigid adherence to the rules of religious dogma have been at the heart of wars, schisms, and societies' prejudice for centuries. We seem no closer to universal peace and understanding now than at the time when religion began. However, for the awakened soul, spirituality transcends dogma. It has little to do with the differences in the way we worship, and has everything to do with human beings evolving as a force for good, and happiness epitomized.

In the words of St Thomas Aquinas, "To one who has faith, no explanation is necessary; to one without faith, no explanation is possible."

AWAKENING TO SPIRITUAL HAPPINESS

There are many and varied paths leading to spiritual awareness and everyone has to find their own way to meaning. Each tradition has its own set of rituals, although at the heart of each doctrine the principles and practice are essentially the same:

- Belief and faith in a higher power
- Time devoted to learning about spiritual matters
- A general belief in our need to love one another as fellow human beings and to strive for a fairer and better world
- Rituals, prayers, or music
- A call for a simple life, free of possessions and the trappings of materialism
- The teaching that we should love others more than ourselves
- A wish to become more connected in universal spirit.

Spiritual awareness for most people means acknowledging something greater than ourselves—a force of love that encourages us to be humble and put the needs of our own ego to one side for others and the common good.

Every so often we are privileged to meet someone who seems to shine with an inner glow, whose kindness and selflessness come not only from the heart, but from a place inside that seems to connect with the greater good and needs of humanity. These are the people who always care about others; whose words of wisdom have a way of soothing trouble and lifting people's spirits; whose faith in something other than themselves seems to fill them with strength in adversity. They have discovered the power of happiness in the art of spiritual awareness.

Spiritual awareness develops in stillness: pause; breathe; listen; look.

SET INTENTIONS

Are you looking to make changes? Is there a part of your life—perhaps your job or where you live—that is causing you unhappiness? Are you frustrated because you never seem to get any closer to realizing your dreams? Or perhaps you'd like to improve an aspect of your personality, such as becoming more patient and tolerant. If so, you can take the first steps by using the power of intention.

Setting an intention is a peaceful and mindful way to sow the first seed of change. It is a way of directing your thoughts toward a desired outcome. If this is done consciously, the intention will transform gradually into a habit of thought that will help change to evolve in a natural way. You may like to combine setting intentions with meditation; when you do this, your higher consciousness takes in the message, which makes it easier for you to allow the change.

SLOW AND STEADY

It's important to break down your intentions into small steps. So instead of setting a big picture intention to "change your career," set a goal to "update my resume," "attend a networking event," or "research courses." As each of your intentions becomes fulfilled, you can move on to the next one.

If your intention is more personal, such as "to improve your relationship with your partner," break it down into an intention to "listen more patiently," "communicate more effectively," "be more tolerant," or "spend Saturday together." Though simple, these intentions are powerful.

EVERYDAY INTENTIONS

Intentions don't always have to be about making big changes and achieving goals. You could wake up each morning and set an intention to be positive, to be kind, or to believe you can handle anything life throws at you.

If, for example, you feel you want a healthier lifestyle, daily intentions can help with this, too. Try setting an intention in the morning to "eat every meal today mindfully" (and you can find out more about this in Week 44) or to "take some exercise," remembering that exercise doesn't have to be a trip to the gym or a three-hour run; it can mean walking around the block at lunchtime, or ending your commute one stop earlier so you walk the rest of the journey. (Find more ideas for simple exercise options in Week 8.)

THIS WEEK... Get started

Begin working on your first intention.
- Break your goal down into small, achievable parts.
- Be specific about each part.

- If possible, set aside time each day to practice meditation, incorporating your intention each time. (If you are unsure of how to meditate, find a class or download an app.)

REFLECT... ON SETTING INTENTIONS

_____
_____
_____
_____
_____
_____
_____
_____
_____
_____
_____

_____
_____
_____
_____
_____
_____
_____

CARE FOR OTHERS

Many parents will say their greatest source of joy and happiness is providing for and loving their children. Mothers undergo a physical as well as an emotional transformation to give birth, which contributes to the special bond of loving care that they feel. For many, the role of father, mother, home-maker, provider, or carer—in whatever form that takes—is not only a personal role, it becomes their main reason for being, and a purpose for life.

Caring for others is a vital part of many people's professions. Nurses, care workers, teachers, and social workers have all chosen professions where the needs of others are the central focal point of every day. Happiness comes, not necessarily from the task, which can be demanding and sometimes exhausting, but from the sense of purpose, the sense of belonging, and the gratitude that is bestowed in return.

Caring for others delivers gratitude in the short term and happiness in the long term. It may take a child their entire lifetime to realize how tenderly they were cared for; an elderly person may be too encumbered by pain to recognize who is looking after them, until the pain subsides; a teacher may never get the thanks he deserves, but may gain satisfaction from students' positive exam results, or from noticing that someone they once taught has risen to professional success.

THIS WEEK: Assess your altruism

How altruistic are you?
- How easy do you find it to put the needs of others before your own? How happy does it make you feel?
- When is the last time you cared for someone, without expecting thanks in return. Did the feeling of well-being outweigh your wish for gratitude?
- Think of three things, however large or small, that you could do for someone today. Write them down, and pledge with a happy heart to do as you say.

REFLECT... ON CARING FOR OTHERS

BEING KIND

One secret of happiness is more effective and more vital to our spiritual well-being than any other, and that is to be kind to others—not just when you feel like it, or because today is world kindness or happiness day, or because you want to feel good about yourself, but because being kind to one another is the only true way for us to find happiness in this world.

In the spirit of John Lennon's song of universal love and hope, imagine what it would be like if everyone was kind, all the time. We are not talking about the home-baked and sugary kind that overindulges and makes us feel slightly queasy. We are talking about habitual kindness; hard to give kindness; being kind before you have received kindness; being kind because it is simply the right thing to do; being kind even if you have a sense of dislike for someone; loving kindness and forgiving kindness.

Kindness lies at the heart of happiness because when we help other people, we feel good about ourselves. Kindness is also an energy for good; those who receive kindness are more likely to give kindness to others in return.

ACCEPT, DON'T REJECT

There are two common barriers to happiness: pride and independence. Sometimes in life, rejecting an offer of help can be a weakness. True success is rarely gained solely by our own efforts—and part of life's pattern includes facing times when we feel vulnerable and unable to cope. By allowing others to "be alongside" during our time of need, we are inviting love and care into our lives.

Sometimes, the most direct path to happiness involves getting out of our own way. This might mean asking others for advice and guidance, receiving help, accepting a kindness that we might never be able to repay, or simply accepting that we can't possibly do it all. Surrender, acceptance, going with the flow—all of these states can be daunting, especially to someone who feels that they are losing control over their life. The irony is that in asking for help or accepting kindness, we are not only receiving, we are giving too. Part of the process of acceptance is to focus on the needs and motivation of the person who wants to give or to help—to enjoy their act of love and kindness, and allow them to be part of your story.

THIS WEEK... Try asking for help

Take a look at how you respond to others when you need help.

- If you find it hard to ask for help, ask yourself why. What is the worst that can happen? Are your fears realistic, or is your pride getting in your way?

- If you hear yourself saying, "I'd love to accept, but I can't because …," check out your true motives. Are you sure you can't? Or are you choosing not to?

REFLECT... ON ACCEPTING, NOT REJECTING

_____
_____
_____
_____
_____
_____
_____
_____
_____
_____
_____
_____
_____
_____
_____
_____
_____
_____
_____
_____

NAVIGATING GRIEF

It may seem odd to have a section on grief in a book that is about happiness, but the reality is that most of us will experience periods of grief in our lives, and sometimes we can get stuck there. We may have the sense that we no longer deserve to be happy because it would in some way be a betrayal of the sadness and depth of emotion we still feel.

This section is included to suggest that choosing happiness is not disrespectful to those we have lost, and it need not diminish the importance or the memory of what has passed. Happiness is the gift that others would wish us to have if they care about us—and the gift that we deserve if we care about ourselves.

The whole of life is about beginnings and endings, happiness and loss. It seems we can't live life to the full without experiencing both states; we can't enjoy one, without encountering the other.

Coping with endings of any sort can be acutely painful. We first learn this in childhood. Perhaps you remember the pain of leaving your neighborhood and friends because you were moving to a new place; maybe your family experienced the devastation of a divorce; perhaps a beloved pet died—or worse, you may have lost someone close to you. In adulthood we may experience love and the pain of break-up several times, and the impact can be devastating. The pain of losing a life partner after many years together may never go away.

Grief carries echoes, so every time we experience a new loss, we are reminded of the losses that have gone before. Sometimes this intensifies our sense of grief, but it may create a sense of numbness in those who choose to button down their feelings and to deny their pain, so afraid are they of the intensity of their feelings. The danger is that their denial or detachment may insulate them from future happiness as well.

THE ART OF ACCEPTANCE

Dr Elisabeth Kübler-Ross was a psychiatrist, author, and pioneer of hospice care. She devoted her entire working life to understanding the nature of death and dying, and identified five states of being that are experienced when grieving:

- Denial: This can't be happening.
- Anger: I am angry at the world because it is happening.
- Bargaining: If I do x, then please don't let y happen.
- Depression: The first stage of emotional acceptance.
- Acceptance: The point at which the grieving person finally accepts the reality of the situation.

It is helpful to recognize these states, because everyone experiences them differently and at a different pace. When in the depths of despair, it can be hard to believe that your feelings will ever shift, and that you might ever experience happiness again. But the reality is, if we are patient with ourselves, it is possible both to accept what has happened and continue to feel love for those you have lost; it is possible to experience new happiness without compromising the strength of the feelings that you had before.

RAISE YOUR CHI

In Traditional Chinese Medicine (TCM) the body's life force and energy levels are known as chi. Our chi levels have a dramatic impact on our well-being and on the organs of the body. When we are feeling happy, our levels of chi increase; the body functions more healthily, and a positive cycle ensues.

In Western medicine, we measure the levels of endorphins, serotonin, dopamine, and adrenaline produced by the body. These, too, increase when we are happy. Together they help us to feel good, look good, and behave more healthily. However, when we are feeling low, the opposite happens. We tend to eat the wrong foods, slow down, and hold tension in the body. Our blood flow slows, meaning the body does not process and expel toxins. The levels of happy chemicals reduce; our levels of chi energy reduce; the body becomes out of balance and we are more likely to feel low, weepy, or depressed.

Many complementary therapies focus on increasing chi levels and getting the body back into balance. Techniques such as aromatherapy, reflexology, reiki, and acupuncture can all be beneficial for releasing energy blocks and easing the mind.

THIS WEEK... Try yoga

If you want to reduce the level of stress and tension in your body while learning to improve concentration and focus, yoga stretches and breath work can be very beneficial. Balancing calm healing processes with regular cardiovascular exercise will shape up the heart and lungs, reoxygenate the blood by making it flow faster and more freely, and trigger the release of "feel good" chemicals, such as dopamine, endorphins, and serotonin.

- Find a local yoga class for beginners to learn the basics.
- Look online for instructional videos to help you practice the techniques.

REFLECT... ON RAISING YOUR CHI

_____
_____
_____
_____
_____
_____
_____
_____
_____
_____
_____
_____
_____
_____
_____
_____
_____
_____
_____

SENSE HAPPINESS

Much of what makes us happy is experienced via our senses. Our sight and senses of hearing, taste, touch, and kinesthetic (physical) awareness send messages to the brain in ways that help us to store and recall memories in milliseconds. A certain perfume might conjure up a favorite friend; the scent of a tree or flower might transport you back to a vacation; the sound of a song on the radio will take you back to the first time you heard that band; the taste of a fruit might remind you of a meal shared with friends; standing in an airport lounge may remind you of standing in a similar spot to meet someone off a plane.

Every day throughout the year, thousands of commuters change trains at Clapham Junction station in south London. It just so happens that several of the platforms face west. So in the fall months, as the evenings begin to shorten, many are treated to a beautiful sunset while they are waiting for a train. The majority of people keep their heads steadfastly downward, focused on sending texts, reading their book or newspaper; but if they were to choose to look up for a moment, they might see something so beautiful that it would soothe away the troubles of the day in an instant.

THE POWER OF THE SENSES

We are used to using speech to express our thoughts and feelings, but stimulating our other senses can summon up all kinds of memories, or can be used simply as an immediate mood changer. Equally, sensory deprivation of any sort will have an impact on how we experience life, and our sense of well-being. Take a moment to answer the following questions:

- What does happiness feel like to you?
- What does it look like?
- What color is it?
- What does it sound like?
- What does it taste like?

THIS WEEK... Boost your happiness

When you think about your current environment, which senses are being stimulated in a way that gives you enjoyment, and which are being starved? Once you understand the memories and triggers that boost your experience of happiness, you can begin to make changes to the way you live.

- If you love music, when was the last time you turned up the volume and played your music loudly enough to appreciate it properly?

- If happiness feels like being close to someone, when was the last time you gave someone you care about a huge hug?
- If you love the taste of food, how often do you cook up a meal for friends?
- If happiness is the color green, can you make time to go for a long country walk?
- If happiness looks like becoming a home owner, what steps do you need to take to make it happen?

REFLECT... ON SENSING HAPPINESS

DISCOVER THE COLOR OF HAPPINESS

Do you have a favorite color? Are you aware of different colors affecting your mood? You may not be aware of it, but the colors you surround yourself with at home and at work, and the colors of the clothes you wear, can impact on your happiness levels.

Color results when lightwaves are absorbed or reflected at different frequencies. Our brain translates the frequencies into the color we see via color transmitters in the eye. Many complementary healers use color as a tool for healing. Bright colors are used to sell products; for example, yellow in particular is used to help house sales.

So why, when we have so many beautiful colors to choose from, do many people insist on wearing black? Black is the color of convenience and funerals—and style. Bright colors, on the other hand, are for carnivals and gardens, summer days and party nights. Colors send a message about our mood and frame of mind.

IT'S SPRINGTIME

In a study from the Vrije Universiteit in Amsterdam to assess how colors affect mood, adults reported feeling happier around green and yellow. Not surprisingly, green and yellow are the colors of sunshine and spring fields, and spring is the season when many people begin to feel more positive and happy. Green is also associated with optimism, as is orange. So really the message is to brighten up your life a little! What have you got to lose?

THIS WEEK... Brighten up!

If you are feeling a bit fed up, resist the temptation to camouflage your mood by wearing black.

- Choose to raise the vibration of your day by wearing something bright and colorful. The chances are, not only will you feel more cheerful, but those around you will also notice and appreciate the splash of brightness, too.

- If you're someone whose go-to color is black or gray because it's just simpler that way and you don't want to buy new clothes, why not at least accessorize with a few bright colors? A brightly colored scarf or bag might just put that spring in your step.

- Take a look at your home. If your walls are magnolia, could you choose to paint one a brighter color? Is it time for a DIY facelift?

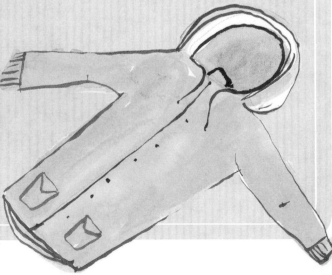

REFLECT... ON THE COLOR OF HAPPINESS

_____

_____

_____

_____

_____

_____

_____

_____

_____

_____

_____

_____

_____

_____

_____

_____

_____

_____

_____

_____

EMBRACE THE MAGIC OF MUSIC

Music moves people. It can uplift and energize as easily as it can trigger sadness or romance. I was once sent a CD as a thank you from a young client. It was a compilation of favorite happy songs from old musicals, and featured tracks such as "The Bare Necessities" and "Singin' In the Rain." My client called it "A Gift of Happiness" and it was. It had me smiling from beginning to end.

According to research, the positive feelings associated with listening to music are due to the brain releasing dopamine, a neurotransmitter that controls the brain's reward and pleasure centers. When you listen to a tune that has an emotional impact on you, the dopamine starts flowing! The study found that even anticipating the sounds of a composition like Vivaldi's "Four Seasons" or Phish's "You Enjoy Myself" can trigger this feel-good chemical. "You're following these tunes and anticipating what's going to come next and whether it's going to confirm or surprise you, and all of these little cognitive nuances are what's giving you this amazing pleasure," said Valorie Salimpoor, a neuroscientist at McGill University in Montreal. "The reinforcement or reward happens almost entirely because of dopamine."

THIS WEEK... Tune in to music!

What would be your top 10 happiness tracks?
- Write them down and add a note on how they make you feel. If they bring back particularly good memories, write those down too.

- Create your own CD compilations and playlists to deliver instant happiness at times when you need a helping hand.
- Spread happiness by creating a positive playlist for someone you care about.

REFLECT... ON THE MAGIC OF MUSIC

_____

_____

_____

_____

_____

_____

_____

_____

_____

_____

_____

_____

_____

_____

_____

_____

_____

_____

_____

LEARN TO SAY NO

If you're a people pleaser, this in itself will bring you a certain amount of happiness. You're someone who gains pleasure from witnessing other people's pleasure and the positive feelings it gives you. The downside to this, however, is that you are quite likely to please them at your own expense. For example, you might not have time to go to a neighbor's birthday drinks, but you agree to go anyway, or you're too busy to help someone move house, but you feel bad about saying no. Agreeing to things you'd rather turn down leaves you less time to focus on your own busy life, and may lead to stress and unhappiness.

People pleasers who say no to things are often left feeling guilty, which can also bring unhappiness. So if this is you, have faith in your friendships: remember that good friends and people who know you well will accept a rejection from you. It won't essentially change how they feel about you.

It can feel very hard to say no, but a simple sentence, such as, "I won't be able to do that for you because I am already very busy/fully committed/doing something else," delivered in an assertive way is enough. Try not to make lots of excuses as this just brings more attention to the fact you're turning down the invitation.

THIS WEEK... Assess your commitments

Take a look back through your schedule for the past six months:
- Look at the things you did that didn't bring you much pleasure or that you really didn't have the time for.

- Look forward to the next six months and fill it with those things you enjoy and people you truly enjoy spending time with.

REFLECT... ON LEARNING TO SAY NO

_____
_____
_____
_____
_____
_____
_____
_____
_____
_____
_____
_____
_____
_____
_____
_____
_____
_____
_____
_____
_____

LEARN SOMETHING NEW

We all have self-limiting ideas about what we can't do or are not good at. Many of these attitudes stem back to our school days where the pathway through exams inevitably led to most of us focusing on what we were good at, rather than on the things we most loved. It's important to let go of any preconceptions about what your skills and talents might be and to open your mind to new experiences and opportunities. We never lose our capacity to learn, grow, and change.

Ken Robinson, British author, speaker, and international advisor on education, is passionate about the importance of creativity in our education systems and in our personal development. He has a heartfelt belief that we each have unique talents and abilities that can inspire us to achieve much more than we currently dream possible. But in order to find out what those talents are, we need to tune into the world of our imagination, our intuition, and our senses, to truly experience and be stimulated by the world. He calls the process of loving what you do and doing what you love being "in your element."

DON'T BE OLD BEFORE YOUR TIME

You can choose to make sure that getting older doesn't become a barrier to happiness. Avoid the mindset that you're too old to learn something new or realize your dreams. Getting older can be a time of liberation, laughter, and fun. Look forward to your future. When you look back, what will you respect about the choices you have made? And what will you

regret that you haven't done? Honor your life by seizing your opportunities. When you make your decisions, don't let age be the excuse that got in your way. Many people begin to live their lives more safely as they get older. Understandably, they feel more physically vulnerable or less energetic. But there are examples all around the world of healthy people in their nineties undertaking brave endeavors, just as there are people in their forties who have already said goodbye to their youth. Have you got a dream that you put to one side when you were younger?

THIS WEEK... Bring your dreams to life

When is the last time you learned something new? Make this the week you start turning your dreams into reality. Learning new skills and acquiring knowledge boosts confidence and makes us happier.

- Take a piece of paper, or use the journal notes page here, to write down things you've always dreamed of doing—don't feel restricted or think of barriers. Just write what's in your heart. For example, have you ever dreamed of learning to skydive, dance, ride a horse, or a motorcycle? Have you had a hankering to learn a language, paint, take up carpentry, or even start a business?

- Now think about what excuses you have been putting in your way. Do you want to look back in years to come and regret that you never tried? Or are you willing to take a risk and stretch your boundaries for the sake of curiosity and the risk of happiness?

- Finally, write down your first action toward achieving your goal. It may be research or it may be seeking advice or telling a friend. When you have done that action, write down your next action, and so on.

REFLECT... ON LEARNING SOMETHING NEW

CELEBRATE YOUR LIFE

When one of my closest friends celebrated a milestone birthday, she decided to invite all her female friends from every stage of her life for one big girly knees-up. Her husband and her children played host and it was a joyous and sometimes riotous evening that grew into a whole weekend. Looking around the room, it was like seeing a picture of different stages of her life in microcosm.

A few months later she was diagnosed with a brain tumor, and she faced that terrifying time with her characteristic positivity and bravery. Fortunately, she has recovered fully and is in fine health once more. But looking back on the ups and downs of her life—and her year—she commented, "I was so happy at my party. I looked around the room at all the friends who were there, and I thought to myself, 'It has all been all right. I have done a good job. My life has been worthwhile. I love my family; my husband and I are still enjoying life together; my children are well balanced and happy, and soon to be embarking on their own lives; and I am surrounded by friends whom I love and who have witnessed my life with all its ups and downs. I have been so lucky, and I am so happy with my life'."

What I loved and respected about her words was her ability to notice and appreciate the importance of that moment. She saw that all the actions and decisions she had taken over the course of her life had led to that moment of recognition and celebration. She hadn't arranged the party as a review of her life; she arranged it to have fun and enjoy the company of friends, and to celebrate a mid-life coming of age. But in taking the time to reflect on that shared moment with other people, she realized how happy she was and that realization help her to embrace the next phase of life, too.

BE PRESENT

Your future happiness begins in the present moment. Yesterday has gone; nothing you do or say can change the past—but tomorrow and the days ahead are unchartered territory. There is so much you can do to influence the way your future evolves and what you feel about it. Living life consciously puts more emphasis on the present moment. It brings our present actions into clear focus; encourages us to mind what we think and to think about what we do and say.

Paying attention to the present moment encourages careful observation and appreciation of the things around us; it puts us in closer touch with our feelings, our reactions, and our intuition, because there are no distractions. By appreciating the present, we can also choose to be happy with this moment—and recognize with every second, every minute, and every hour that passes that we are right here, right now, and can influence the future—in any way we choose.

AWAKEN YOUR SENSES

Your senses send messages to the brain. When your senses are alert, you feel more alive. Focus fully on what you are doing at every moment of the day. There is joy to be had in every task: the sight of a robin hopping about while you are weeding; the smell of the ingredients while you are baking; the sound of your children chattering while discovering their world; the hug or touch of a friend or lover. Appreciating the small things awakens awareness of the bigger things, and helps to put us back in touch with our true selves.

MINDFULNESS

By being more present—more mindful of the present moment—we can learn to let go of the need to control our experiences. We can become more compassionate toward ourselves and more accepting of how things are. It is not about trying to stop things or change them and this acceptance can, in itself, make us more relaxed, calm, and happy. Some will find it possible to get more pleasure and happiness out of everyday chores by tuning into them and focusing on the positive experience, instead of dreading them and just wishing they were over. So, yes, you really can be happy doing the vacuuming!

THIS WEEK... Try mindful meditation

Try either or both of these meditations to help you stay relaxed and present. Allow any thoughts that come into your mind—they're quite normal—and just gradually bring your attention back to your breath. Don't criticize or judge your wandering mind.

- Make sure that both feet are firmly on the ground and move your attention to the soles of your feet. Imagine that you are breathing in and out through the soles of your feet. Continue for a few breaths or for as long as you wish.

- Sitting or lying in a relaxed position, focus on your breathing and notice where you feel the breath most strongly—for

example, in your chest or lower down in your belly. Notice the sensations of breathing. You may want to place a hand on your chest or belly. As you watch your breath, stay with the length of the in-breath—follow it through. Then do the same with the out-breath. Do this for as long and as often as you wish.

REFLECT... ON BEING PRESENT

_____

_____

_____

_____

_____

_____

_____

_____

_____

_____

_____

_____

_____

_____

_____

_____

_____

_____

_____

_____

_____

CHOOSE TO BE OPTIMISTIC

Professor Martin Seligman has devoted his professional life to reframing the way that psychology is used and viewed. He has been at the forefront of the concept of "positive thinking" and his work has developed the field of psychology so that it focuses as much upon making well people happier as it does on influencing those with depression or other conditions.

His research has found that there are three main types of happy life:

- The pleasant life. Finding as many ways as possible to create a life of pleasure; seeking positive influences and developing positive emotions to enhance our experiences in life.
- The good life. Living a life of engagement—via our work, or by finding purpose in raising a family; knowing what your strengths are and using them to live life in a state of flow.
- The meaningful life. Using your unique skills and talents for the greater good.

A life of engagement and meaning is enhanced by pleasure; but a life of pleasure alone is not the most successful route to finding happiness. This is because we become used to the feeling of pleasure. The initial feeling of euphoria diminishes when the pleasure is repeated without a sense of personal engagement or meaning—just as the first chocolate out of the box tastes delicious and leaves us wanting more but eating the whole box at one sitting diminishes the memory of the first taste and leaves us feeling uncomfortable into the bargain.

Martin Seligman has found that the difference between optimists and pessimists lies in their view of how long the effect of something negative is going to last. A pessimist believes that the impact will last a lifetime, whereas an optimist believes that the effect is time-bound in the short term and may not impact on outcomes in the future.

THIS WEEK... Turn a negative into a positive

This task will be harder if you're a natural pessimist, but that's all the more reason for doing it!

- Think back to a negative experience and write down something good that came out of it. For example, being made redundant may have set you on a different and better career path; reluctantly moving to a new area may have led you to make new friendships; leaving a relationship may have brought out a strength in you that you didn't realize you had; being ill may have led you to make positive lifestyle changes.

- It takes about 30 seconds for a thought to enter our deeper consciousness, so don't give those negative thoughts any time to properly register. This gets easier with practice and can be enhanced with meditation. Every time you think of a negative thought this week, turn it on its head. See the positive affirmations technique on page 164 for more help with this.

REFLECT... ON CHOOSING TO BE OPTIMISTIC

_____

_____

_____

_____

_____

_____

_____

_____

_____

_____

_____

_____

_____

_____

_____

_____

_____

_____

USE IT OR LOSE IT

Think of happiness as a bottomless pot of joy, talent, hope, and gratitude. The more you use it; the more you give to others, the further you spread its contents—the happier you will feel. Using our capacity for compassion and kindness strengthens our energy for living and our joy for life. The pot will continue to remain filled to the brim.

If you disregard your pot of happiness, it will begin to evaporate. The less you use, the more you try to conserve only for yourself, the more anger, resentment, and gloom enters the pot—the faster happiness will fade away.

OUR INFLUENCE

We live life at such a fast pace that we rarely find time to take stock, or stop for long enough to realize the effect we are having on others. But if you start to pay attention to the things you say throughout the day, you will start to notice your impact:

- Do those around you start to smile? Or do they frown?
- Are you lifting people's spirits, so they notice their own skills and gifts? Or do they feel deflated and worried by what you say?

The words we use and the tone we choose has an effect on the people we meet and spend time with, in every moment of every day.

THIS WEEK... Spread a little happiness

Make it your mission to make people smile, no matter how unlike smiling you may feel. If, when you leave, their eyes are shining, the chances are you will have had a positive impact on the next person they meet as well.

- Smile at someone: if you smile, they might very well smile back!

- Say what you see: Go out of your way to pay someone a compliment. It could make a big difference to their day, especially if they are not in a happy place. Realizing you've made someone happy will make you feel happy too!

REFLECT... ON USING IT OR LOSING IT

_____

_____

_____

_____

_____

_____

_____

_____

_____

_____

_____

_____

_____

_____

_____

_____

_____

_____

APPRECIATE NATURE

Spending time in nature is one of the most powerful anti-depressants available to us—
it's free for all and provides an easy route to a happier life.

Breathing sea air, trekking through a shady forest, walking along a towpath, or simply visiting a local park are all ways to get close to nature. City dwellers will of course need to make more effort to get a nature fix, but it's a journey worth making.

HEALTH AND HAPPINESS

Humans weren't meant to live in confined air-conditioned or centrally-heated places. It's unnatural and unhealthy to stay indoors for long periods of time but increasingly children, especially, are tied to activities that limit the amount of time they spend outside. This makes them more likely to gain weight and causes them to be deficient in Vitamin D due to a lack of exposure to sunlight.

Scientists in Japan monitored the effects of a practice known as Shinrin-yoku, which means forest-bathing. For the study, half of the participants were sent into a forest, and the other half into a city. The next day, they swapped places. Those who returned from the forest were found to have "lower concentrations of cortisol, lower pulse rate, and lower blood pressure." A walk in the woods can have even greater health benefits than keeping you fit and reducing stress. There is evidence that chemicals emitted by plants, known as phytoncides, help to strengthen immunity.

THIS WEEK... Discover the great outdoors

Plan a nature discovery weekend:
- Check your local area for green spaces and plan a visit.
- Slowing down and walking quietly will allow you to become fully mindful of your surroundings and to notice plants and wildlife.
- Turn off your cell phone—you don't need to announce your nature trip on social media. Just live in the moment.

REFLECT... ON APPRECIATING NATURE

_____
_____
_____
_____
_____
_____
_____
_____
_____
_____
_____
_____
_____
_____
_____
_____
_____
_____

ASK THE UNIVERSE

Who has not at some point in their lives been struck by an extraordinary coincidence that has transformed their life? One second you are making a wish and the next second the opportunity is there in front of you, as if by magic. These are the moments where the idea of having a guardian angel feels tangible and it appears as if the Universe is very much taking care of our needs. "Be careful what you wish for," friends might say, or "Ask, and the Universe will provide."

Many people hold an instinctive belief that if we focus with good heart and are clear about what we want to achieve, we can manifest our own reality. This process has been called many things over the centuries: it is one of the functions of prayer, it is commonly referred to as the law of attraction, and has more controversially been termed the "cosmic ordering service."

COSMIC ORDERING

The popular German author Bärbel Mohr was the first to coin the phrase "cosmic ordering," the idea being that if we focus fully on the things that we want in life, they will appear and our fortunes can change. The law of attraction, similarly, focuses on the power of our thinking. If we see things in a negative light, we will attract negativity into our world. On the other hand, if we project a very precise and positive vision of what we would like our future to be like, the Universe will conspire to help to make this happen. The idea that we can influence outcomes with the power of our thoughts is seductive—provided we use such influence for the common good. All too often, however, the process is used for material gain (cars, possessions, etc.) rather than personal growth.

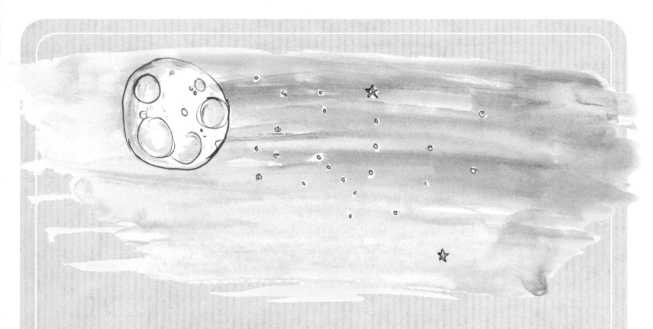

THIS WEEK... Visualize your dreams

Picturing what you want may just bring you a step closer to getting it.

- Visualization meditation: Sit comfortably, close your eyes, and relax into a meditative state, then visualize the things that you want. If any negative thoughts and doubts come to mind, try to sit with them without judgment and allow them to pass. Then bring your mind back to your visualization.

- Make a vision board: Download or photocopy images that represent your goal and stick them to a board. This process will help you clarify and focus on what you want to be, do, or have in your life. Display the board somewhere prominent in your home.

- If you struggle with this, or get "stuck" in dark thoughts, please stop, or ask a professional for help with moving through your troubled state.

REFLECT... ON ASKING THE UNIVERSE

_____

_____

_____

_____

_____

_____

_____

_____

_____

_____

_____

_____

_____

_____

_____

_____

_____

_____

_____

_____

NOURISH YOURSELF

We all know that the quick fix that comes from eating junk food and sweet treats is a false pleasure. Feelings of sluggishness may quickly lead to regrets and self-recrimination. Nourishing your body with the right foods and eating them more mindfully can beat sugar cravings and set you on the path to well-being.

Healthy eating, rather than dieting, is the desired intention. Time and again extreme diets have been shown not to work. Instead, by eating well and being more mindful about food preparation and planning, you will naturally cut down on calories and give yourself a nutrient boost. A healthier, happier you is the most important goal.

FOOD PLANNING

A great way to start is by clearing out your kitchen cabinets, refrigerator, and freezer. Put them in some sort of order and throw out those dodgy cans that are past their expiry date. By stocking up on the essentials, all you will need to do is top up with purchases of fresh food.

The secret of success is forward planning, week by week, for meals that give you a good, overall balanced diet. It's advisable to shop after you have eaten to avoid those hunger pangs leading you to impulsively purchase comfort foods.

FOOD PREPARATION

Be mindful as you prepare food, whether that's putting spread on your toast or cutting up vegetables. Noticing the smells, textures, and even sounds of food is said to improve your digestion and enhance your appetite.

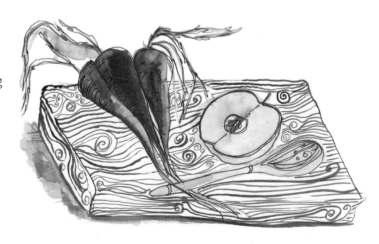

EATING MINDFULLY

If you're someone who barely sits down to eat, or you wolf down your food in a few minutes, it's time to take stock. Your body isn't being given a chance to respond to what you're consuming and may be in a state of stress. Rushing meals hampers digestion and is more likely to lead you to overeat.

Eating mindfully can help you to understand your relationship with food:

- First notice whether you are in fact hungry. By being in tune with your body and its hunger signals, you'll eat when you need to rather than out of habit.
- Becoming mindful of portion size and presentation on the plate may help you to choose a healthy amount.
- Before you begin eating, remove distractions—turn off the TV, put your phone out of reach. Now really look at the food and take in the colors, shapes, and smells. When you eat it, notice the taste and texture and take your time, chewing every mouthful thoroughly. Learn to recognize the signs that you are full so that you don't overeat.
- If you tend to undereat, take time to present the food well. Pay attention to textures and flavors that you enjoy. Eat with friends.

Be kind to yourself and be patient. Over time, and with help and support if necessary, it is possible to change our relationship with food.

THIS WEEK... Plan ahead

Tune in to the triggers that lead you to eat high fat or high sugar foods:

- Be aware of how you're feeling emotionally and be aware of any physical sensations in your body. Recognize what is happening but don't judge yourself.
- Bring your attention to your breath: breathe in and out a few times or until your attention shifts.
- Again, assess how you are feeling both physically and emotionally before making your choice.
- There is no right or wrong choice but by giving yourself space to think, you can make a mindful decision.

REFLECT... ON NOURISHING YOURSELF

_____

_____

_____

_____

_____

_____

_____

_____

_____

_____

_____

_____

_____

_____

_____

_____

_____

_____

PRACTICE SELF-COMPASSION

It may seem a bit clichéd to say "be your own best friend," but it's actually very good advice. When you treat yourself with the same loving kindness and compassion you give to friends and family, you start to feel happier in your own skin.

When someone close to you is feeling down, perhaps about some aspect of their appearance or about their progress at work, it's natural to want to lift their spirits. You'll no doubt quickly find something positive to say and put the problem in perspective, leaving your friend less worried and more confident. Like most people, you may not be quite so wise and understanding when it comes to yourself.

GIVE YOURSELF A BREAK

In our celebrity-driven culture we are bombarded with images of people who appear to have it all. It's not surprising that so many people are left feeling inadequate in comparison, but what we often discover is that these so-called "successful people" are far from content. True happiness develops when we accept ourselves as fully rounded human beings, and acknowledge our weaknesses as well as our strengths, then understand, forgive, and find the positives in those weaknesses. So, for example, if you're "too sensitive," is it part of the same trait that makes you very caring?

THIS WEEK... Be your own best friend

- Write a letter to yourself, explaining an aspect of yourself or your life you are unhappy with. Express your feelings fully—no one else will read the letter.
- Now write a letter from an imaginary friend, who is compassionate and fully accepting of all your faults. This friend understands why you are the way you are and all the history that led to this point.
- As you read the letter, accept the love and care and try to introduce this level of self-compassion into your life.

REFLECT... ON PRACTICING SELF-COMPASSION

THE GIFT OF LOVE

When two people share an intensity of feeling, the heart sings and they may feel capable of anything. The feeling of being loved is a true gift and it really does make us feel happier, but not all kinds of love are sustainable, and when love changes its form, we cannot demand that someone loves us back in the same way.

Much of life is about loving and losing and learning how to give and take in relationships. When a relationship ends it can feel as if life is over and that you will never laugh, smile, or be ready for love again. Unrequited love can be equally painful, leaving the person who feels unloved consumed with a sense of loss that can become debilitating and sometimes self-destructive. Love is a gift that can bring as much pain as it does joy. It can take courage to pick yourself up, dust yourself off, and start all over again.

But, of course, your love was never *your* love. We do not belong to one another. We cannot be owned. What we can do is share moments in time that send the heart soaring and bring us to life; we can choose to grow old together or part with the memory of precious moments that we can treasure for a lifetime.

"LOVE DOES NOT CONSIST OF GAZING INTO EACH OTHER'S EYES, BUT LOOKING TOGETHER IN THE SAME DIRECTION."

ANTOINE DE SAINT-EXUPÉRY (1900–1944)

CHOOSING LOVE OVER SADNESS

- Love is not a finite pot of feeling. There is always room for more. Instead of telling yourself that you will never love anyone ever again, try thinking, "I will never stop loving the person I have loved. Even though I am in pain at the moment, my heart is open to loving someone new in time."

- Spend time with friends and family who love and appreciate you. Although their kindness may make you more acutely aware of the one you are missing, their support can help you to accept what has passed and move on.

- Time passes. There is a cliché that time heals all things, and in the case of loss and heartbreak it is true. One day you will wake up to find that something has shifted. You feel free to be yourself again. Instead of wanting to hang on to what you had, you will see why you had to let it go. Trust in the process and you will find your way back to happiness.

EROS: LOVE ETERNAL

The Ancient Greeks believed that erotic love was a form of madness. The Greek god, Eros, is characterized by his bow and arrow, as he shoots painful darts into the hearts of those afflicted by passion. But interestingly, the concept of eros as a form of love has nothing to do with physical beauty. Whereas physical beauty fades, eros is considered to be eternal—which just goes to show, happiness, like beauty, is more than skin deep.

POSITIVE AFFIRMATIONS

Using affirmations daily is a powerful but simple way to bring happiness into your life. Much of what makes us feel low stems from the negative chatter that runs through our mind daily. Affirmations shut down this chatter and give us a happiness boost. Over time, with repetition, your go-to thoughts will become more positive.

It's important that your affirmations are in the first person and present tense. For example, "I am confident," "I am healthy." If you hear yourself think or say passive words, such as "I wish," "I should," "I might," "I can't," swap them for more active words: "I can" or "I am." Your choice of language puts you in control of your life.

REPEAT, REPEAT, REPEAT!

Your negative chatter can be a tough opponent. Let's face it: it has been around for a while and is well-practiced. By diverting your attention toward positive affirmations, you will gradually feel more hope-filled and happy. That's why it's important to practice affirmations daily—ideally for at least 21 days in a row. One technique is to stand in front of the mirror and state them repeatedly. Or, if you prefer, you can write them on post-it notes and stick them around the house. Do whatever works for you. When you're out and about, perhaps for a walk or a run, repeat them silently.

THIS WEEK... Choose daily affirmations

Choose one affirmation for each day, focusing on areas of your life or aspects of your personality you want to improve. It's important to believe in your affirmation as if it is already 100 percent true.

- Initially, write down the affirmation five times.
- Read it back to yourself five times.
- Next, stand in front of the mirror, looking yourself in the eye, and say the affirmation five times. You may be self-conscious about this, but each time you repeat the phrase your mind will become more positive.

REFLECT... ON POSITIVE AFFIRMATIONS

_____

_____

_____

_____

_____

_____

_____

_____

_____

_____

_____

_____

_____

_____

_____

_____

_____

_____

_____

DISCOVER YOUR INNER CHILD

Children seem pre-programmed for happiness. They are liable to catch a bout of happiness very quickly and take great delight in passing it on. Most young children are happiness magnets. All they need is love, safety, and space to play to create a world where fun is but a laugh and a smile away.

Children have the power of imagination to help if something happens to ruin their day. They quite simply take themselves off to a happier place! Children talk in superlatives— and they really notice the details. When something is in favor, it is immediately "best" or "favorite" and essential to life (although things may fall out of favor just as quickly). Can you still remember your favorite childhood toy, picture book, or TV program?

WHEN LIFE GETS IN THE WAY

As they grow older many people lose the happiness habit; they swap fun and spontaneity for personal responsibilities and replace play and imagination with the routine of work and a busy diary. Pressure of time leads to living life in a rush; true happiness becomes a rare commodity saved for weekends, vacations, and special occasions.

THIS WEEK... Return to childhood

Take some time to think back to your childhood years, perhaps a specific vacation or a special relationship with a friend.

- Close your eyes and allow yourself to visualize that time. Can you see yourself laughing, being silly, having fun? Were you creative and adventurous?

- Now open your eyes and write down on a piece of paper what you visualized.
- What three key words would you use to describe yourself then?
- What aspects of your childhood self would you like to bring back into your life now?

REFLECT... ON YOUR INNER CHILD

_____
_____
_____
_____
_____
_____
_____
_____
_____
_____
_____
_____
_____
_____
_____
_____
_____
_____
_____
_____
_____
_____

DIGITAL DETOX

A digital detox is a period of time during which you live without using digital devices, such as smartphones and computers. It is an opportunity to reduce stress and to focus on social interaction in the physical world rather than through technology.

It's fairly well documented that being tied to our digital devices 24/7 doesn't make us happy. In fact, an unhealthy level of dependency on technology has countless negative effects, including an increased likelihood of anxiety, stress, and insomnia. Having social media on tap encourages narcissism on the one hand and feelings of inadequacy on the other, as every aspect of daily life is photographed, shared, and compared online. Constant communication in text-speak and via email can take its toll on "real" conversation and leads to social isolation for some. We don't allow ourselves downtime because the technology allows us to respond immediately. Research has found that on average we spend the equivalent of three weeks every year on social media and checking email—that's an entire annual vacation!

A DIGITAL DETOX EXPERIMENT

A recent study was carried out by a company called Kovert, who are researching how technology is changing people's behaviors and bodies. In this experiment, a group of 35 CEOs and entrepreneurs were taken on a trip to Morocco to study their behavior with and without technology. They spent the first day in a hotel, where they had full access to technology, and the following four days in the desert, without any of their electronic devices. Throughout their stay they were observed by undercover neuroscientists. These were the results:

- After three days there was a noticeable change in their posture. They looked forward more than down; they made more eye contact.
- Without access to Google they found out their answers to the trivial questions that come up in conversation by discussing them. This led to deeper, better, informed, longer conversations because they weren't cut short by searching online.

- They remembered more details about the people they were with, simply because they were paying more attention during the conversations.
- They all slept better.
- Some of the group made important decisions about how they wanted to change their career or relationship; others decided to improve health and fitness. A lack of access to technology had given them time to focus on the things that really mattered.
- They all decided that they wanted to introduce a digital detox into their everyday lives.

In another study, researchers at the University of Kansas sent 56 people on hiking excursions in the wildernesses of Alaska, Colorado, Maine, and Washington. The participants were not allowed to use any electronic devices. The result was an increase in creativity, overall attention, and problem-solving abilities.

THIS WEEK... Power down your tech

Going on a full digital detox may be something you need to work up to gradually, but here are some simple ways to reduce your overall tech time:

- Put your phone on mute, so that it does not buzz or ring to distract you.
- Set yourself a maximum daily allowance. For example, allocate one short time slot in the evening to check social media, instead of being distracted from more important tasks and people.
- When you are at home in the evening, put your phone away in a drawer. Only look at it once you've spent proper time with loved ones, eaten your evening meal, etc.
- Turn off all technology two hours before bedtime and make your bedroom a tech-free zone.
- On waking, don't check your phone until you are dressed, have eaten your breakfast, and have spent some time with your family.
- Try to make one day per week a full digital detox day.

REFLECT... ON YOUR DIGITAL DETOX

_____

_____

_____

_____

_____

_____

_____

_____

_____

_____

_____

_____

_____

_____

_____

_____

_____

_____

_____

_____

_____

DISCOVER HYGGE

Denmark regularly comes top in the United Nations World Happiness Report,
so it may be worth paying attention to what the Danes feel is the key to happiness.
It comes in the form of *hygge* (pronounced hoo-gah)—put simply,
hygge is about focusing on the pursuit of happiness by embracing and
enjoying the small pleasures in life.

The dictionary definition of hygge is "a quality of coziness and comfortable conviviality that engenders a feeling of contentment or well-being." Meik Wiking is CEO of the Happiness Research Institute in Copenhagen; he says the key ingredients of hygge are togetherness, presence, relaxation, and comfort. It's about coziness and family time, and fully appreciating and not feeling guilty about having downtime. What's not to like?

BECOME MORE HYGGE

So how can you get a bit more hygge into your life? Think slow, think natural, think craftsmanship and comfort. Here are a few tips from Meik Wiking:

- It's essential to create a cozy atmosphere at home where you can comfortably indulge in your hygge lifestyle. Forget plastics and think ceramics. Forget steel and plastic and think wood. Imagine creating your own log cabin indoors.

- Create your own perfect cozy, self-indulgence kit, complete with snuggly socks, candles, soothing herbal teas, and good-quality chocolate. This isn't for one-off cozy nights in; this is an everyday indulgence and self-care routine.

- Get crafty by knitting or doing other creative pastimes. When we create something we have to be focused and mindful—this will naturally take us to a

more relaxed and pleasurable place where we can leave everyday worries behind.

- Who wouldn't get pleasure from the smell of freshly baked cakes and pastries, or a delicious smelling casserole on the stove? Hygge is all about home-made, rustic cooking. Nothing fancy, nothing perfect—just something made with love that can be shared with others.

- Hygge is a very sociable concept that can be shared and enjoyed with others. Hygge activities tend to involve friends, perhaps a weekend away, a trek in the woods, or a cozy movie night. Anything that will encourage relaxation and togetherness.

- Finally, be thankful for all those wonderful small pleasures in your life. Wiking says, "Research shows that people who feel grateful are not only happier but also more helpful and forgiving and less materialistic. It's all about savoring simple pleasures."

THIS WEEK... Make your home more hygge

When you enter a home that is hygge, it will immediately feel comfortable and cozy. This atmosphere is very simple to create:

- First, turn down those bright lights. Choose either natural daylight or candlelight. You can use candles anywhere and everywhere. Even better, if you're lucky enough to be able to combine it with light and warmth of a roaring fire.

- Add a few soft furnishings: woven throws, a sheepskin rug, and chunky knit pillows are all so inviting. Who wouldn't want to cozy up and get all hygge on the sofa?

- When friends visit, turn off the TV and spend quality time together. If you're properly hygge, you'll have baked something simple that's filling your home with wonderful aromas. Don't forget to offer a cozy hot drink—think hot chocolate with marshmallows or a glass of mulled wine. If you're making lunch or an evening meal, do so together. Hygge is all about communal cooking, sharing, and togetherness.

REFLECT... ON DISCOVERING HYGGE

_____
_____
_____
_____
_____
_____
_____
_____
_____
_____
_____
_____
_____
_____
_____
_____
_____
_____
_____

BE MORE LAGOM

Lagom is a Swedish concept, referring to moderation. Loosely translated it means "not too little, not too much, just right." The idea is to find happiness and contentment by adopting a more balanced and frugal approach to life.

People often kick back at the weekend by excessively indulging in their pleasures, especially after a hard week at work—for example, they might go out late to a bar, eat a huge takeout meal, or stay in bed an hour too long in the morning. While these activities may be pleasurable at the time, there may be disadvantages, too, in the form of a hangover, weight gain, and a lack of time to get things done.

LIVING MORE LAGOM

Lagom is the complete antithesis to these extremes—with lagom you won't over-indulge and although you might not have those highs, you certainly won't have the lows. Everything will feel just right in your world.

Lagom is not about being ostentatious about what you have—your clothes, your car, your home—but instead about being quietly confident and contented. When you go out for the evening, you are part of the group but not the life and soul of the party. There's no pressure to deliver, no pressure to have the best night of your life—you are simply one part of the whole, and there's something very relaxing, sustainable, and stress-free about that.

THIS WEEK... Find more balance

Look at your overall routine and lifestyle and assess where you could find more balance.

- Are there lifestyle excesses you could cut back on?

- Which areas of your life could you potentially declutter?
- How can you create a better work/life balance for yourself?

REFLECT... ON BEING MORE LAGOM

_____
_____
_____
_____
_____
_____
_____
_____
_____
_____
_____
_____
_____
_____
_____
_____
_____
_____

BE YOUR AUTHENTIC SELF

You may know someone who seems to be consistently cheery and wonder how they manage to sustain that level of happiness. How does he or she manage to remain so positive? Is it an act? Is it possible to be happy all the time and still be true to yourself?

Most people at some point or another will mask their true feelings or may compromise their own needs for a peaceful life. This is natural, especially in unfamiliar situations—but living your entire life this way can be tiring, stressful, and ultimately soul-destroying. When we drop the mask, we let go of many of our fears too, because we become true to ourselves.

LIVING A MORE TRUTHFUL LIFE

Having the confidence to live authentically evolves over time. Every decision, from career path to fashion style to choice of friends, beliefs, or life partner, leads to greater self-knowledge, and ultimately to the contentment that comes with self-acceptance:

- You know who your true friends are because you can always be yourself with them.
- You find pleasure in your work for its own sake.
- You are not afraid to voice your opinion, even when you risk dissent.
- You have the courage to remove yourself from situations that are bad for you.

THIS WEEK... Put your true self first

Try to be honest with yourself about areas of your life that are not fitting your needs.

- Do you attend social events you don't really enjoy? What would you rather do?
- Do you put up with, rather than enjoy your work? Is there a path that you would find more fulfilling?
- Are you making compromises in a relationship? How might you change this?
- Which of your life goals is the most important to you right now? Knowing this, what will you choose to do next?

REFLECT... ON BEING AUTHENTIC

_____
_____
_____
_____
_____
_____
_____
_____
_____
_____
_____
_____
_____
_____
_____
_____
_____
_____

REFLECT ON YOUR HAPPINESS

In reaching the final weekly activity, I truly hope that the ideas and action points have inspired you to arrive at a happier place.

It can take time to realize that much of the joy and happiness we experience originates from our own heart, mind, and soul. It is possible to create personal happiness. The seeds are planted in the thoughts, dreams, and actions of every day.

LOOK BACK... AND FORWARD

Flick back through the book, over the full 52 weeks, and use the checklist on page 186 to work out those activities that suited you best and were most effective. Only you can know what your idea of happiness looks and feels like. Read back through any notes you made for each week. You may also wish to make a note of your happiest events and memories of the year on pages 184–185.

As you have browsed through these pages, whether occasionally or week by week, some ideas will have resonated more than others. I truly hope that you will have been inspired to seek your own pathways, too.

THIS WEEK... Declare your happiness

It can help to spend time focusing consciously on the kind of future you would prefer. Try completing the following statements:

- I am happiest when...
- My happiest memories are of...
- The people who make me happy (and who I need to show appreciation to) are...
- My future vision of happiness looks like this...
- My actions for happiness are...
- I deserve to be happy because...

You may well find that your answers change and evolve over time.

REFLECT... ON A YEAR OF LIVING HAPPILY

_____
_____
_____
_____
_____
_____
_____
_____
_____
_____
_____
_____
_____
_____
_____
_____
_____
_____

HAPPINESS AT YOUR FINGERTIPS

These pages bring together thoughts and suggestions from throughout the book. They are repeated here so that you can dip in to remind yourself of some of the ways you can re-anchor yourself. If you want to take a more intuitive approach, close your eyes and let your finger land anywhere on the page, then take on board the idea for the day!

Review your well-being. Reflect on those areas of your life that you may have been neglecting. What have you been putting off that would lighten your heart and increase your well-being?

Set yourself new challenges. Like a plant that has been pruned or newly planted, we sometimes grow most vigorously when we have been knocked back or choose to begin life anew.

Make happy plans. We schedule our work, and we note birthdays and other key events on the calendar, but few people choose to set themselves goals for life. Deciding what you want to achieve, where you want to go, and what you want your legacy to be can be very empowering. Begin with just one thing.

Respect your need for a routine. Everything in the natural world has a rhythm. It varies subtly with the seasons, but there is a pattern to each day.

Look after your health. Your body and mind are connected. You will feel less strain if you look after your physical self, and take care that you have enough sleep, food, and exercise.

Treat yourself with respect. Sometimes, when we are unhappy, we may take revenge on ourselves by treating ourselves badly, by diminishing who we are, or becoming angry and pushing others away.

Believe in yourself. Self-belief increases our ability to achieve the outcome we seek.

Take action. If you have a goal, choose to commit to it. Focus on changing the things you can.

Seek acceptance. For those things that you can't change and that are beyond your control.

Become true to yourself. Happiness lies ultimately in our ability to accept ourselves as we really are.

Appreciate the contrasts in your life. White looks whiter when it is seen next to black than it does when it is next to gray; times of joy are more intense when you have experienced times of sadness.

Be patient. There are times when life presents a challenge that is so painful and unexpected that it may feel as if you will never experience happiness again. Developing patience and understanding are the pathways to hope. It is possible to rediscover joy in time.

Let go. Of your need for control, for perfection, of your expectation that life should be lived completely on your terms.

Use the language of happiness. When you use words such as joy, contentment, glee, delight, bliss, gladness, fun, merry, you send positive and upbeat signals to other people that lighten their hearts.

Seek guidance. If you are struggling, reach out to someone who can help you through the tough times; for some that may be a friend, for others a coach or counselor, for others a higher power.

Be kind—to yourself and others. Kindness and happiness are partners through life. Where one leads, the other always follows.

Acknowledge your feelings. Happiness is not something you can buy from a store; it doesn't turn up on demand; it comes from the heart and may appear when you least expect it.

HAPPY EXPERIENCES AND MEMORIES

_____
_____
_____
_____
_____
_____
_____
_____
_____
_____
_____
_____
_____
_____
_____
_____
_____
_____

CHECKLIST OF ACTIVITIES

Mark off activities as you've completed them, and perhaps make a note of ones that particularly helped you. You can then refer to this list when looking for ideas on ways to enhance your happiness.

☐ **Week 1**
Look for Happiness

☐ **Week 2**
Live Simply

☐ **Week 3**
Find Happiness at Work

☐ **Week 4**
Value Who You Are

☐ **Week 5**
Let Go of Fear

☐ **Week 6**
Hug More!

☐ **Week 7**
Communicate Consciously

☐ **Week 8**
Shape Up for Happiness

☐ **Week 9**
Sleep Well

☐ **Week 10**
Avoid the Moan Zone!

☐ **Week 11**
Become Less Complacent

☐ **Week 12**
Stop Procrastinating

☐ **Week 13**
Surround Yourself with Positive People

☐ **Week 14**
Learn to Forgive

☐ **Week 15**
Escape Loneliness

☐ **Week 16**
Deal with Negative Feelings

☐ **Week 17**
Be More Curious

☐ **Week 18**
Appreciate Your Uniqueness

☐ **Week 19**
Think Like a Lottery Winner

☐ **Week 20**
Discover the Art of Giving

☐ **Week 21**
Be Still and Calm

☐ **Week 22**
See the Funny Side of Life

☐ **Week 23**
Do Something Creative

☐ **Week 24**
Take a Risk

☐ **Week 25**
Nurture Your Friendships

☐ **Week 26**
Spend Time with Animals!

☐ **Week 27**
Take Pride in Your
Appearance

☐ **Week 28**
Put Yourself in Another's
Shoes

☐ **Week 29**
Discover Loving Kindness

☐ **Week 30**
Set Intentions

☐ **Week 31**
Care for Others

☐ **Week 32**
Accept, Don't Reject

☐ **Week 33**
Raise Your Chi

☐ **Week 34**
Sense Happiness

☐ **Week 35**
Discover the Color
of Happiness

☐ **Week 36**
Embrace the
Magic of Music

☐ **Week 37**
Learn to Say No

☐ **Week 38**
Learn Something New

☐ **Week 39**
Be Present

☐ **Week 40**
Choose to Be Optimistic

☐ **Week 41**
Use It or Lose It

☐ **Week 42**
Appreciate Nature

☐ **Week 43**
Ask the Universe

☐ **Week 44**
Nourish Yourself

☐ **Week 45**
Practice Self-Compassion

☐ **Week 46**
Positive Affirmations

☐ **Week 47**
Discover Your Inner Child

☐ **Week 48**
Digital Detox

☐ **Week 49**
Discover Hygge

☐ **Week 50**
Be More Lagom

☐ **Week 51**
Be Your Authentic Self

☐ **Week 52**
Reflect on Your Happiness

FURTHER RESOURCES

There is a plethora of books, videos and other resources available on the science and roots of happiness, but here are a handful that I found inspiring while researching this book.

BOOKS

Achor, Shawn *The Happiness Advantage* (Virgin, 2011)

Bienkowski, Andrew *One Life To Give* (Experiment, 2010)

Buzan, Tony *Embracing Change* (BBC Books, 2005)

Csíkszentmihályi, Mihály *Flow: The Psychology of Happiness* (Rider, 2002)

Dalai Lama, The and Howard C. Cutler *The Art of Happiness* (Rider, 1998)

De Saint-Exupéry, Antoine *The Little Prince* (Egmont, 1991)

Ferrucci, Piero *The Power of Kindness* (Tarcher, 2007)

Frank, Anne *The Diary of Anne Frank* (Pan, 1969)

Frankl, Viktor *Man's Search for Meaning* (Rider, 2004)

Gerhardt, Sue *Why Love Matters* (Routledge, 2004)

Gibran, Kahlil *The Prophet* (Arrow, 2005)

Gilbert, Dan *Stumbling on Happiness* (Vintage, 2007)

Hamilton, David R. *Why Kindness Is Good For You* (Hay House, 2010)

James, Bev *Do It! or Ditch It* (Virgin, 2011)

Kaufman, Barry N. *Happiness is a Choice* (Ballentine, 1991)

Long, George (trans) *The Meditations of Marcus Aurelius* (Duncan Baird, 2006)

Milne, A.A. *Winnie-the-Pooh* (Methuen, 1926)

Mountain Dreamer, Oriah *The Invitation* (Thorsons, 1999)

O'Donohue, John *Anam Cara* (Bantam, 1999)

Pilkington, Doris *The Rabbit-Proof Fence* (Miramax, 2002)

Rao, Srikumar *Happiness at Work* (McGraw-Hill, 2010)

Robinson, Sir Ken *The Element* (Allen Lane, 2009)

Rubin, Gretchen, *The Happiness Project* (HarperCollins, 2009)

Seligman, Dr Martin *Flourish* (Nicholas Brealey, 2011)

Siegel, Daniel *Mindsight* (Oneworld, 2011)

Zander, Benjamin and Rosamund Stone *The Art of Possibility* (Penguin, 2006)

RESOURCES

The search for Authentic Happiness is ongoing at Penn State University. Those who want to take part in the survey can register for free via the Authentic Happiness website and complete a series of questionnaires: www.authentichappiness.sas.upenn.edu

The Pursuit-of-Happiness project includes an online quiz and a series of in-depth questionnaires to monitor and measure factors affecting happiness. Visit the happiness quiz at: www.pursuit-of-happiness.org

The Kindness Calendar can be found at www.maketodayhappy.co.uk and offers suggestions on a kind act to undertake every day.

The TED: Ideas worth spreading website contains many illuminating videos on a huge number of diverse subjects. Visit the website at www.TED.com. This is a very short list of the talks I most enjoyed:

Achor, Shawn "The Happy Secret to Better Work," February 2012

Csíkszentmihályi, Mihály "Flow: The Secret to Happiness," October 2008

Gilbert, Dan "The Surprising Science of Happiness," September 2006

Rao, Srikumar "Plug Into Your Hard-wired Happiness," March 2010

Robinson, Sir Ken "Ken Robinson Says Schools Kill Creativity," June 2006

Robinson, Sir Ken "Bring On the Learning Revolution," May 2010

Seligman, Dr Martin "The New Era of Positive Psychology," July 2008

Zander, Benjamin "The Transformative Power of Classical Music," June 2008

REFERENCES

Many of the opening quotes were sourced from www.goodreads.com. Original sources are included here where it has been possible to research them:

Page 10: The Declaration of Independence can be accessed via The National Archives, www.archives.gov

Page 11: More recent data can be found at www.happiness360.org

Page 12 on Bhutan was influenced by an article in the *Independent* magazine by Andrew Buncome, 14 January 2012

Page 15: The Happy Planet Index is at www. happyplanetindex.org

Page 15: Helliwell, J, Layard, R, & Sachs, J, *World Happiness Report 2017*, New York: Sustainable Development Solutions Network (2017)

Page 39: The fear-busting exercise is adapted from an approach used by Bev James in *Do It! or Ditch It* (Virgin, 2011)

Page 47 refers to Rimer J, Dwan K, Lawlor DA, Greig CA, McMurdo M, Morley W, Mead GE. "Exercise for depression." *Cochrane Database of Systematic Reviews* 2012, Issue 7. Art. No.: CD004366. DOI: 10.1002/14651858.CD004366.pub5

Page 84: Mackenzie, Susan, "Sharing the Wealth: *The Sunday Times* Giving Index," June 2007, issue 29

Page 154: Bärbel Mohr (1964–2010) was the author of *The Cosmic Ordering Service* (Mobius, 2006) and other titles

ACKNOWLEDGMENTS

Behind the words on the page are many others who helped to create this book: in grateful acknowledgment of conversations with the inspiring and talented people and professionals whose views and knowledge helped to shape the content—in particular, the fabulous Bev James, for her constructive and energizing encouragement. My great appreciation to Cindy Richards, Carmel Edmonds, and the team at CICO Books for their tremendous skill and creativity—with special thanks to Dawn Bates, who wrote additional text and created ideas and activities, especially for weeks 9, 13, 23, 26, 27, 30, 42, and 44–51. Lasting thanks, too, to Clare Sayer, Helen Ridge, Anna Galkina, Marion Paull, Amy Louise Evans, and Emily Breen. With huge love and thanks to my family and friends—and in loving memory of my wonderful mother (the original Lois), whose love of life was always inspiring.

INDEX